100 Years of Scottish Sport

100 Years of Scottish Sport

Edited by RODGER BAILLIE

MAINSTREAM
PUBLISHING

EDINBURGH AND LONDON

To Rosemary, Andrew, Michael
and Louise

First published in Great Britain in 1994 by
MAINSTREAM PUBLISHING COMPANY (EDINBURGH) LTD
7 Albany Street
Edinburgh EH1 3UG

ISBN 1 85158 666 0

A catalogue record for this book is available from the British Library

Typeset in Stempel Garamond by Servis Filmsetting Ltd, Manchester
Printed in Great Britain by Butler and Tanner Ltd, Frome

Contents

How it All Began

Introduction

The *Daily Record* started its sports coverage with a bang! The newspaper burst into life on Monday, 28 October 1895, with full coverage of Scotland's league matches.

It was a sports editor's dream come true. The headline on the lead story split the Old Firm. 'RANGERS AT EDINBURGH' wasn't exactly an inspired choice but underneath was the real story: 'Phenomenal Display of Celtic against Dundee. Record League score.' The anonymous reporter, under the pen-name 'Bedouin', told in the lead story of Celtic's 11–0 crushing of Dundee at Parkhead:

'The annals of Senior League contests in both Scotland and England may be searched, and searched in vain, for a parallel to the extraordinary event which transpired at Celtic Park on Saturday, the return fixture between Celtic and Dundee. Nothing approaching it has ever transpired in connection with the game in Scotland.

'Fresh from triumphs over such redoubtable opponents as Heart of Midlothian and Rangers, the visitors were expected to emerge from this contest with some degree of merit but, strange to say, they tumbled completely to pieces and went down at the ropes. Historians have been furnished with fresh figures, for there is nothing in the calendar which will bear comparison with the sensational victory of the Celtic Football Club. Eleven goals to none forms a record score for the Scottish League.'

It was all there, plus quotes from Celtic and Dundee players telling of how the Tayside club, reduced by injury to nine men, had been crushed completely.

Such a score is rightly still a 'phenomenon', but a century later, although the styles of the players have changed and the financial rewards of 1994 would have built a fleet of battleships for the ever-growing Royal Navy of 1895, there are everlasting themes which a time-traveller from this century would find familiar. For example, a refereeing row enlivened that Monday morning one hundred years ago. Here is the verdict on controversy in the 1–1 draw between Hibs *v*. Rangers at Easter Road:

'When Rangers were awarded an equalising goal not a few cheered them because they felt they were entitled to a point. It could not have been because they admired the goal, for it wasn't a goal at all, the ball going through off a post from a corner kick, though, in the opinion of the referee, breasted through by one of the Rangers. However, the point was allowed, much to the Hibs' disgust, and the game was resumed amidst intense excitement.'

The SFA, surprise, surprise, were under attack:
'The legislators of the SFA meet tomorrow night when no doubt the usual crop of protests, rough-play cases and professional irregularities will come up for settlement. Possibly also there will be a repetition of recent scenes with the chairman, for some of the gentlemen who sit around the horseshoe are not afraid to openly assail Mr Harrison's right to the position of his conduct as guide of the meeting. Such exhibitions are in very bad taste.'

Nor have the problems for punters diminished in one hundred years. In 'Racing Chat' the meeting at Windsor was spotlighted and 'Mornington' sighed, 'The eccentricities of handicappers know no limit.' And so through the years the *Daily Record* has gone on to report the moments of joy, and the days of gloom, on Scotland's sporting stage – and the rest of the world.

This book is a pick-and-mix choice of some of these memorable moments. The ranks of the papers for the last century stand bound together in the filing-cabinets of the *Record*'s Anderston Quay headquarters in Glasgow. They are proud, silent testimony to the effort put in by so many people over the years – the named writers and the sub-editors toiling behind the scenes – to make sure every week-day morning the readers of Scotland's biggest paper get the best possible sports service, both entertaining and accurate.

In the years just prior to the paper's birth, massive steps were taken particularly in football to shape the outline of the sport as it is today. After a long and bitter debate, professionalism was approved in 1893, and the heyday of the first great club of Scottish football, Queen's Park, was almost over. The following year Celtic won the League Championship but lost to Rangers in the Scottish Cup final. The Old Firm rivalry had truly started.

Tucked away beside the major events that excited the readers are the stories of Rangers' first Cup win in 25 years in 1928, the largest crowd ever in Britain at the Scotland *v.* England clash at Hampden in 1937, and Celtic's European Cup win in 1967. The rise and fall of boxer Benny Lynch and the only time an Olympic Games event was held in Scotland, when yacht races took place on the Clyde in 1908 as part of the Olympiad staged in London that year, are gems to be mined.

It is, of course, impossible to squeeze all the happenings from a hundred years into one book. This is a look at the highlights, as reported at the time by the paper. For each event and each personality I have selected, the text is the same as it was when the readers bought the paper that particular day. The writing has not been changed: it is the *Daily Record* of the times they lived in. I hope you enjoy it.

RODGER BAILLIE

Field of Dreams

Scottish Football Memory Lane

Success and failure, joy and anguish; the *Record* has been at the heart of Scottish football for a century, cataloguing the progress – or lack of it – in the country's national sport. Here is the *Record* of Monday, 7 April 1902. 'The Clyde emigration season is in full swing,' reported the paper, informing its readers that two ships had sailed for Canada with a total of 1,850 emigrants on board, 'many of them of North-East farming stock.'

But there was no doubt about the main news. Under the heading 'APPALLING CATASTROPHE' was described the first Ibrox disaster, when part of the west terracing gave way during the Scotland *v.* England international attended by 70,000 people. Apart from a lack of pictures, the reporting is as full as if it had taken place yesterday, with perhaps a little more literary flourish, as was the style of the era.

'What was expected to have been one of the greatest football matches ever witnessed between the chosen representatives of England and Scotland became in the sequel the most memorable in the annals of the game – memorable, unhappily, not because of the play, but for an appalling calamity which occurred a few minutes after the kick-off.

'The match was being played on Saturday on the Rangers ground at Ibrox Park, in the outskirts of Govan, about two and a half miles from the centre of Glasgow. A portion of the high terracing at the west end of the ground gave way, with the result that several hundred people were precipitated to the ground from a height of about 40 feet.

'Over 270 in all received injuries necessitating their being medically attended to in the infirmaries or elsewhere; three were dead or practically upon the point of death when lifted; and since then 15 others have succumbed to their injuries, making a death toll up till last midnight of 18.'

In fact, the final death toll was 25, and 587 received compensation for their injuries. One victim graphically told the paper that when the terracing collapsed spectators had been flung into the hole created 'like coal being tipped out of a cart'.

'It was quite apparent long before three o'clock that the terracing all around the track, no less than grandstands, was too crowded to admit of any more being safely accommodated. Still newcomers pressed in at every avenue and the spectacle soon became something more than impressive – it became alarming.

'The accident happened when fans swayed forward to see a corner kick. John Drummond, a cabinetmaker from College Street, Aberdeen, said: "The last thing I saw was Livingstone heading towards the English goal with the ball at his toe and the first, on regaining consciousness, was the walls of the Western Infirmary. My fall must have been broken by some of the victims for I've only an injured wrist. The doctors say I have had a miraculous escape."'

Many of the victims were taken to the city's Western Infirmary in horse-drawn ambulances, crossing the Clyde by the Govan horse ferry. 'A gentleman who witnessed the scene described it as one never to be forgotten.' The unnamed writer who covered the match said:

'It was a tremendous spectacle, at first gladdening, latterly imposing, and finally awful. For who can forget the surging of the human waves on the fated terracing, the sudden gap in that portion which gave way beneath the over-pressure of the crowd tossed to and fro, the wild waving of handkerchiefs for assistance by those in front, and the lamentable procession of injured and dying being carried away.

'The game went on primarily to avoid a perhaps worse scene, because it would have been quite impossible for the people to have had their admission refunded to them and because at the time the full extent of the accident was neither realised nor known.

'Nicol Smith, of the Scottish team, said that not one single player on the field had the slightest idea the accident was so serious until they retired as usual to their dressing-rooms at the interval. "It quite sickened most of us" he said, "as we stepped over the prostrate forms of the victims on the pavilion floor. I never saw such a sad scene in my life, and I hope never to see another."'

The paper added: 'Mr Wm Wilton, the manager of the

The men who played in the Ibrox disaster match, 1902. The line up is back row (left to right): J. Wilson (trainer), R. Walker (Hearts), N. Smith (Rangers), J. Doig (Sunderland), A. Kirkwood (President, SFA), J. Drummond (Rangers), A. Raisbeck (Liverpool), R. Dixon (treasurer), J. Robertson (Rangers). Front row: R. Templeton (Aston Villa), A. Brown (Spurs), A. Aitken (Newcastle Utd), G. Livingstone (Celtic), A. Smith (Rangers).

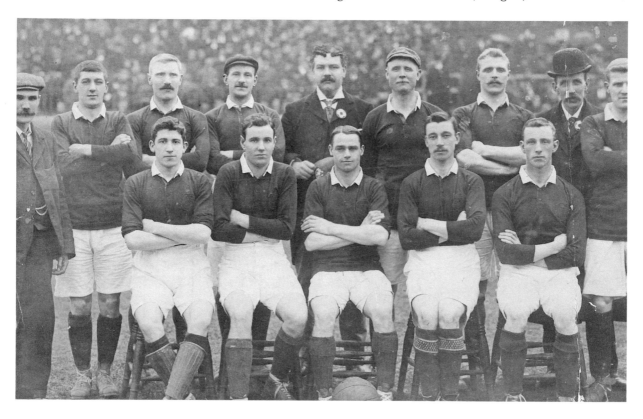

Rangers ground, was quite overcome by the awful calamity that had taken place.' It was the end of wooden-style terracings, a disaster waiting to happen.

The match ended in a 1–1 draw, and it was declared an unofficial international. The two countries met a month later at Birmingham and drew 2–2. The Exhibition Cup, played for a year earlier to celebrate the Glasgow Exhibition, was renamed the British League Cup and top teams from both sides of the border competed for it to aid the relief fund for the victims. Celtic won it, just as they were to be triumphant in two other similar trophies later in the century, the 1938 Empire Exhibition trophy and the 1953 Coronation Cup.

Football history repeated itself at Ibrox in a grimmer way. On 2 January 1971, at the Ne'erday Old Firm fixture between Rangers and Celtic, 66 fans were killed on the ill-fated Passageway 13 at the Rangers end of the ground. Of the dead, 32 were teenagers, and the paper pictured one of them, 16-year-old Brian Hutchison from Barlanark, Glasgow, in his bedroom with the wall covered with Rangers posters. 'For him Rangers was almost a way of life. It was also, unhappily for him, a way of death. He was one of the Rangers fans who did not come home.'

The tragedy happened when Jimmy Johnstone's goal in the final minutes of the game was equalised by Colin Stein. Donald Bruce wrote vividly:

'The disaster at Ibrox Park on Saturday is the worst we have ever known in British sporting history. Even now we cannot appreciate its ghastly finality. The magnitude of horror as pathetic body piled on top of pathetic body in an unstoppable stampede of death on a stairway. Ninety minutes before, 66 people had climbed that same stairway full of New Year cheer, happy and excited at the prospect of what has always been a feast of football from Glasgow's biggest clubs, Rangers and Celtic.

'An hour and a half later, they were dead – 66 of them – suffocated, as anonymous Rangers fans, hearing about Stein's last-minute equaliser, went back up the stairs to meet the thousands coming down the stairs. Somebody tripped and fell. The rest piled on body after body and the iron stanchions broke; there it was in all its simple, stark, awful horror – disaster at the big game.'

I retain the awful memory of looking down that Saturday

night from the heights of the Ibrox press-box, then perched on the roof of the stand, to the ghastly scene of 66 bodies laid out on stretchers behind the goal at the Copland Road end of the ground. Sadly, I was to report on another, worse, disaster for the *Record*, at the Heysel Stadium in Brussels. And Britain produced more black-bordered episodes, with the Bradford and Hillsborough disasters.

Rangers, after 1971, took the decision to rebuild their stadium. The man responsible was manager Willie Waddell, who pushed the scheme through for approval by a board of directors paralysed by the events. Ibrox today is a memorial to Waddell, and to those 66 fans who died on that dreadful afternoon, not just another Saturday.

Old Firm games have produced some of the greatest matches in Scotland's football history, and some of the blackest chapters. Sadly, violence has too often been linked to these games and two of them, 71 years apart, produced scenes which rocked football to its foundations.

On Saturday, 17 April 1909, Prime Minister Herbert

Day of remembrance: Rangers players and officials lead the homage to the 66 fans who died in the 1971 Ibrox disaster. From left to right: the Rangers team, chairman John Lawrence, directors Matt Taylor, George Brown, Ian McLaren and David Hope, manager Willie Waddell, coach Jock Wallace and trainer Tommy Craig.

Asquith was addressing a meeting in Glasgow, talking about the introduction of Old Age Pensions, and Fred Karno's Comic Company, of which Charlie Chaplin was a member, were top of the bill at The Hippodrome. And the Old Firm were meeting in a Scottish Cup final replay at Hampden. There are some differences between then and now. The paper said loftily on the eve of the game, 'Nothing fresh has transpired with regard to the Scottish Cup final.' That changed dramatically, in a game that became notorious as the battle of Hampden. It's best described in the sparse language of the police report on the scenes, which the *Record* published as part of its massive coverage of the riot.

'Inspector McKay of this division reported that at the finish of the football match between Rangers and Celtic Football Clubs, in Hampden Park, Mount Florida, and directly after the referee had blown his whistle announcing the finish, the Celtic team remained on the field as if with the intention of playing an extra half-hour, the Rangers team leaving the field. The Celtic team shortly afterwards followed. The spectators being under the belief that an extra half-hour would be played, remained in their position.

'The Football Association, in the interval, decided that the game for the day would be finished, and would not be renewed. The spectators, on being informed of the decision, held on and demanded that the game should be renewed and, their wishes not being complied with, they invaded the playing pitch.

'The police endeavoured to restore order and to get the crowd to behave peaceably, but the rowdy element amongst them would not listen to reason, and came on with force, overwhelming the police. They commenced to tear up and wreck the woodwork around the enclosure and tear down the goalposts, using them as weapons against the police.

'The utmost disorder prevailed. The crowds attacked the entrance gates and turrets in Somerville Drive, setting them on fire. The Queen's Park Fire Brigade was called out, but had great difficulty in extinguishing the fire, owing to the interference of the crowd, who pelted them with stones and missiles.'

The *Record*'s reporters portrayed the scenes vividly. 'It

was a battle royal between police and hooligans', 'unparalleled scenes of brutality', 'disgraceful exhibition', 'the most fiendish outburst of inflamed passion ever seen in a civilised country'. The battle between the police and the mob lasted for two hours. Unusually for the time, there was a picture of the players on the pitch at the end, obviously unsure whether there was going to be an extra thirty minutes.

The unnamed leader-writer of 1909 wrote vehemently about football hooliganism in a theme that was to become depressingly familiar down the ensuing years. 'A Disgrace to Glasgow,' trumpeted the paper. The Scottish Cup was withheld for the only time in its history. The men who took part in that match were the only players never to receive either winner's or runner's-up medals for their endeavours.

The Rangers players that day were Rennie, Law, Craig, Gordon, Stark, Galt, Bennett, McDonald, Reid, McPherson, Smith. And Celtic, the backbone of whose side won six consecutive League titles, were Adams, McNair, Weir, Young, Dodds, Hay, Kivlichan, McMenemy, Quinn, Somers, Hamilton.

Saturday, 10 May 1980, was to go down in Scotland's soccer history as the second battle of Hampden, and again it involved a clash between Celtic and Rangers. As early holidaymakers were taking off for two weeks in Corfu for £113, Old Firm fans fought a pitched battle on the Hampden turf after Celtic striker George McCluskey had scored an extra-time winner. The paper reported:

'The trouble started when Celtic fans spilled from the east terracing to acclaim their cup-winning heroes, climbing the six-foot-high fence to do so. Then raging Rangers fans swept over the fences at their end and the battle was joined. Showers of bottles, stones and cans rained on to the field. Battling fans armed with iron bars and wooden staves, ripped from terracing frames, created the most violent and ugly scenes at Hampden in more than 70 years. Mounted police with drawn batons galloped across the pitch, separating the rival fans and herding them back on to the terracings.'

And Page One told the story of 'the Hampden heroine', detailing how 22-year-old PC Elaine Mudie on her grey gelding, Ballantrae, had braved a hail of missiles to try to clear battling fans from the pitch. She made history by becoming the first woman mountie in Britain to be involved in a full-scale charge with batons raised to disperse rioters. 'It was a nightmare trying to dodge the flying bottles and cans. I was pretty scared, but we had a job to do, and Ballantrae was magnificent. As we left the ground the fans in the stand stood and applauded. It was a touching moment – I was in tears,' said PC Mudie.

For all of us at the *Record* it was an event which hit home even more than usual, as one of our colleagues was in the firing line. Sports photographer Eric Craig was among the most severe casualties. He suffered a fractured skull when he was struck by a bottle as he snapped the scenes on the pitch. Even today he has a legacy of that awful afternoon, suffering slight deafness in his right ear from the mindless action of a mindless hooligan. Reporter Alex Cameron was in no doubt as to where the blame lay.

'How many more disgraceful scenes have to be endured before Rangers honour a promise which could make a start towards ending the bigotry bedevilling Scottish football?

'The louts from both ends of Hampden who soiled the Cup final with savagery were motivated by hate. Forget, for a moment, the arguments about who started the mayhem, or how it could be prevented. The root cause is religion. And while no one would suggest that one club is solely to blame, Rangers stubbornly refused to do their part in a modern way to start the long and difficult process of removing this horrible barrier.'

Both clubs were fined £20,000 by the SFA. But, more importantly, the outcome of that dreadful afternoon was long overdue Government legislation. The Criminal Justice Bill (Scotland) is a mouthful for any football fan to say. But its impact was as far-reaching as any club take-over, more important than any star transfer. Among the many provisions it made, it outlawed supporters taking alcohol into sports grounds, or carrying drink on supporters' coaches and trains. The effect was dramatic and immediate. The game was changed for the better. Vigilance can never be relaxed, but hopefully riots like those that scarred football will not be repeated.

Triumph and tragedy are never far from the sidelines at Old Firm matches, such as Rangers' triumph in 1928. Incredible as it may seem now, the Ibrox club had gone 25

At last: Rangers with the Scottish Cup after their 1928 win over Celtic ended 25 years of failing to win the trophy. Manager Bill Struth (centre) is holding the Cup.

years without winning the Scottish Cup. They had piled up League titles, but the Cup had eluded them since they had last won it in 1903.

They met Celtic in the final on 14 April 1928, in front of a crowd of 118,115, desperate to see if the Ibrox Cup hoodoo would be swept away. In those days an incredible 108,090 paid at the gate, and only 10,025 were advance tickets. 'Waverley' began his report with the words of the Ibrox club's chairman:

Back from Canada: the Rangers line-up of 1930 just off the boat train at St Enoch Station, Glasgow.

'At last, "at long last", as ex-Bailie J. Buchanan said at the cup presentation ceremony in the Queen's Park FC Reading Room, Rangers have laid the bogey that has haunted them for a quarter of a century. I saw the elusive trophy carried off in triumph to Dumbreck on Saturday night.'

The decisive goal was scored from a penalty 11 minutes into the second half. Waverley described it:

'From a Morton centre the ball was fired in by Fleming and Thomson was beaten. But out the ball came from off a Willie McStay hand and, of course, Ibrox claimed a penalty or a goal – or both? And a penalty Willie Bell granted, and granted rightly, after a consultation. Davie Meiklejohn picked a place for it, and Rangers led in the 11th minute.'

That was the turning-point, as Rangers went on to win 4–0 with further goals from Bob McPhail and two by Sandy Archibald. But it was Meiklejohn's penalty that was acclaimed. If he had missed Celtic would have got the boost to send them surging to victory, but instead it was Rangers who had adrenaline pumped into them.

'Brigadier' was in the Rangers dressing-room at the end. It was the nom-de-plume of John Allan, who was later to have a spell as editor of the paper. Other executives of that pre-war era believed he tilted the paper's coverage too much towards Ibrox. Still, he obtained a series of quotes – unusual in those times when players were seen but rarely heard, as the journalists of the day tended to give maximum space to the views of directors and other officials.

'"You sunk the penalty like an icicle, man" I told Davie Meiklejohn. "Icicle!" he said. "Why, I never felt so anxious in all my life. It was the most terrible minute of my football career. I hadn't time to think what it would have meant if I had missed, and I can tell you I was relieved when I saw the ball in the back of the net."'

Readers were also told that Bob McPhail claimed his lucky suit had helped make sure the team won. The paper revealed the Cup had been taken on stage at the Princess's Theatre (now the Citizens). For the last 18 weeks comedian George West had paraded a mock Scottish Cup on stage in the *King O' Clubs* pantomime (didn't pantos run for a long time then), and now he was able to show the real thing.

The teams who competed were *Celtic*: Thomson, W. McStay, Donoghue, Wilson, J. McStay, McFarlane, Connolly, A. Thomson, McGrory, McInally, McLean; *Rangers*: T. Hamilton, Gray, R. Hamilton, Buchanan, Meiklejohn, Craig, Archibald, Cunningham, Fleming, McPhail, Morton.

But on 7 September 1931 it was a very different report on another Old Firm game. Waverley described one of Scottish football's greatest individual tragedies – the death of 22-year-old John Thomson, the Celtic keeper, who had won four Scottish caps. Under the heading, 'A LIFE FOR A SAVE', he wrote:

> 'In the midst of life we are in death. At Ibrox on Saturday afternoon we saw John Thomson full of life and virility, truly a splendid specimen of vigorous young manhood: at 9.25 he breathed his last. Poor John.
>
> 'My sympathy goes out to the bereaved mother and father, his sisters and brothers, and to his sweetheart, who saw him as he lay unconscious in the Ibrox pavilion

Up for the Cup: Celtic skipper Jimmy McStay is hoisted on his team-mates' shoulders after the 1933 victory against Motherwell. Goal-machine Jimmy McGrory, scorer of the only goal, is on the extreme left. Manager Willie Maley is second right, front row.

Who'd be a referee! A back view of one of Scotland's most famous, Peter Craigmyle, chased by Celtic players Scarff and Thomson round the goalposts after he refused a Parkhead penalty claim in the 1933 Cup final against Motherwell.

before being taken to the ambulance *en route* to the Victoria Infirmary.

'Hesitating just a fraction of a second as he saw Sam English come on, John threw himself at the ball and the Ranger and the Celt went down. The ball was deflected past the Parkhead right-hand post – Celtic were defending the eastern goal. John Thomson had made one of the greatest saves of his life, but, most unfortunately, it cost him his life. To avert a score he realised that to go out was the only way, and thus the tragedy.

'What a pity! John Thomson was a most likeable, a loveable young man.'

The game ended in a no-scoring draw.

That same season Motherwell broke the Old Firm's astonishing 27-year monopoly of the League title. The *Record* devoted a page to their title-winning achievement. 'MOTHERWELL'S DAY OF VICTORY' was the main headline. And underneath the subheadings stated: 'An epic struggle – years of steady progress – the men who did. Reward of steady, fearless policy.'

There was a picture of the manager, John Hunter, and praise for the skipper, Bob Ferrier. 'Old Original' wrote:

'Motherwell's epic struggle for the League Championship honours has been one of the bright spots for the past six seasons. Now that they have successfully overcome the Old Firm monopoly they must be hailed as worthy champions.'

The 1930s was the era of giant attendances, with records that still stand to this day. In two successive Saturdays in April 1937, Hampden housed incredible crowds of 149,547 for the international against England, and then 147,365 for the Cup final between Celtic and Aberdeen.

The nation's attention was turning towards the Coronation of King George VI the following month, with the news columns full of details of rehearsals for the event in Westminster Abbey. However, all the crowds who saw those games in that Coronation year hardly seemed to have got value for money. There's a sharp contrast in the reports of the two games. Waverley wrote after the international, on Monday, 19 April, when he gave the crowd as 149,407:

'That was the number of people who passed the turnstiles at Hampden on Saturday in a drizzle of rain, to make a thrilling spectacle, to give a wonderful background to the world's greatest football contest. The more one thinks of it the more one marvels at the hold the game of soccer has on the public. It seems almost incredible.

'I think the proudest man I met on Saturday was SFA secretary George G. Graham, wearing a bowler hat at a jaunty angle. He was entitled to be a proud man. He had staged the greatest event in the history of the game and the organisation was perfect. Everything went smoothly, and the great crowd was dealt with in the easy manner of an ordinary Saturday afternoon gate. The public responded loyally to the appeals made to them and the huge bowl that is Hampden filled steadily and surely at an even pace that caused no flurry, no anxieties to those responsible for the promotion.'

Scotland won the international 3–1. The team was Dawson (Rangers) Anderson (Hearts), Beattie (Preston), Massie (Aston Villa), Simpson (Rangers), Brown (Rangers), Delaney (Celtic), Walker (Hearts), O'Donnell (Preston), McPhail (Rangers), Duncan (Derby). Frank O'Donnell and Bob McPhail, with two, scored the goals and no one could have dreamed it was to be the last victory at home against England in an official game until 1962.

Yet only a week later, the same columnist, wrote about the speeches at the after-match reception following Celtic's 2–1 Cup final win:

'Surely the speakers could not have known of the trouble that was engendered by the poor packing of the crowd, the disappointment that was occasioned by the closing of the gates in the face of the thousands, and of the anger of many who tried to force their way through to see the game.

'I spoke to many officials afterwards, and I gathered in no uncertain manner that we have seen the last of pay-as-you-arrive Cup finals. As with the international game with England, so with the last stage of the national trophy competition. Admission by ticket only.

'On the lower part of the terraces there was so far as I could see room to spare. On the higher reaches it looked to me as if greater comfort could have been found in an overcrowded cattle truck.

'The police made every effort to bring the spectators

Snapshots from the '40s. Moscow Dynamo keeper Tiger Khomich recovers from injury during the famous 1945 battle against Rangers at Ibrox. The Rangers players are Torry Gillick, Charlie Johnstone, Billy Williamson and Jimmy Duncanson.

down nearer the track, but it was a hopeless task. In many parts, I learned when making inquiry, it was an absolute impossibility to move, so tightly were patches of the crowd wedged together.'

Celtic's win against Aberdeen was the fifteenth time the Cup had been lifted by the Parkhead club. In those days the trophy was presented to the chairman of the winning club. Waverley described the scene:

'When, in the Hampden pavilion after the game, SFA President James Fleming called upon Mr Tom White to accept the Cup, the Celtic chairman rose and drew his hand across his brow. "Ladies and gentlemen," he remarked in a low voice, "I am tired." Next to me a lady whispered to her friend, "Poor man, without doubt he has been up all night worrying about the game." Mr White looked round the audience. "I am very tired," he continued, "taking away this Cup from Hampden for my club."'

What his Parkhead successors of today would give to be able to say the same! It was manager Willie Maley's 69th birthday, the perfect present for the grand old man of Parkhead. At the after-match celebrations were such old-timers as Jimmy

Quinn and Patsy Gallacher – rated the best Celt of all time by former chairman Sir Robert Kelly.

The teams were: *Celtic*: Kennaway, Hogg, Morrison, Geatons, Lyon, Paterson, Delaney, Buchan, McGrory, Crum, Murphy. *Aberdeen*: Johnstone, Cooper, Temple, Dunlop, Falloon, Thomson, Beynon, McKenzie, Armstrong, Mills, Lang.

The glamour match that signalled the end of the war was the visit of the mighty Moscow Dynamo to Ibrox in November 1945 as part of their British tour. The Nuremberg trials of the top Nazi leaders were being held, but in Scotland the sole topic of conversation was how to get a ticket for the Dynamo game. If Rangers had been playing men from Mars there couldn't have been more interest. Waverley wrote:

'Nothing like it has been known. Just think of this. At one time during the morning there were seven trunk calls queued up – from London, Birmingham, Sheffield, Manchester, Aberdeen and Inverness. All had the same pleading tone: tickets, tickets. Manager Bill Struth produced one letter which made him laugh. "For heaven's sake send me six enclosure tickets for the coalmen. My fire's out."'

Over 90,000 fans packed Ibrox to see a 2–2 draw. The

Off on their travels. Rangers line up before a 1945 trip to Germany, and a 6–1 hammering from a British Forces Select. Left to right: Manager Bill Struth, Alex Venters, Willie Waddell, director George Brown, trainer Arthur Dixon (standing), David Gray, Ian McColl, Dougie Gray, Jerry Dawson, director Alan Morton, Scot Symon, Jock Shaw, Willie Woodburn, Charlie Johnstone, Jimmy Duncanson, Billy Williamson.

Russians went 2–0 up, and Willie Waddell missed a penalty. Centre-forward Jimmy Smith pulled one goal back, and George Young scored with a second penalty. Davie Meiklejohn, by then a journalist with the *Record*, lauded the Rangers centre-half:

'If I single out Young for special praise, it is only because he was the main gear round which the auxiliaries worked. He never let himself be drawn out of position. He stood there as the unpassable sentinel.'

The official Rangers history claimed that Dynamo were guilty of 'pushing and elbow work, body-checks and so forth'. Waverley agreed:

'Nobody minds good, honest robustness. Rangers took a lot and gave something back, but there was more than robustness from certain of the Dynamos. If you ask Jock Shaw he'll tell you, if he feels like it. When he was lying on the ground in pain, it wasn't any ordinary mishap. It was something you don't put in print.

'Had the Dynamos been satisfied to play the game as we are accustomed to see it played Rangers would have done the same. As it was Rangers would have been number-one fools to

The Famous Five together again: a 1979 nostalgic get-together at Easter Road of the legendary Hibs front-line of Gordon Smith, Bobby Johnstone, Lawrie Reilly, Eddie Turnbull and Willie Ormond.

Clown prince of Celtic – but Charlie Tully, for once, is in serious mood before the start of a 1949 Old Firm game at Ibrox. Following him on to the pitch are Pat McAuley, Bobby Collins and John McPhail.

take it like lambs, and not give it back.'

The one amusing incident came after the start of the second half when the street-wise Torry Gillick called over the referee. He had noticed that the Russians had put on a sub, and not taken another player off. They were playing with twelve men.

The Rangers team that November afternoon was Dawson, David Gray, Shaw, Watkins, Young, Symon, Waddell, Gillick, Smith, Williamson, Johnstone.

Elsewhere on the page of the Dynamo match report, Albion Rovers' team against Cowdenbeath was given. The number five was listed as Stein. He would eventually move permanently to top of the bill as Celtic and Scotland manager.

The immediate post-war League Championship campaigns were dominated by two clubs, Rangers and Hibs, the Ibrox side winning four titles and the Easter Road team three. It was the last fling of line-ups that fans instantly recognised, before the squad system that started in the 1960s took over and managers started playing guessing-games with the media and fans. Rangers strength was based on their 'Iron Curtain' defence – Brown, Young, Shaw, McColl, Woodburn, Cox – and Hibs on the flair of their 'Famous Five' forward line: Smith, Johnstone, Rielly, Turnbull, Ormond.

Celtic had a brief flurry of success in the early 1950s, with

Stepping out: Celtic celebrate their 1954 League and Cup double with a trip to Turnberry. The group includes Mike Haughney, Sean Fallon, Johnny Bonnar, John McPhail, Jock Stein, Neil Mochan, Bobby Evans and Charlie Tully.

their half-back line-up of Evans, Stein and Peacock, the foundation stone of the team; and Hearts won the Scottish Cup in 1956 – the first time in 50 years – with a strike-force dubbed 'The Terrible Trio': Conn, Bauld and Wardhaugh.

The four British football associations, Scotland, England, Northern Ireland and Wales, rejoined FIFA in 1947, and a gala match was staged at Hampden.

Post-war crowds boomed and 134,000 saw a Rest of Europe Select play a Great Britain side which consisted of Swift (England), Hardwick (England), Hughes (Wales), Macaulay (Scotland), Vernon (Northern Ireland), Burgess (Wales), Matthews (England), Mannion (England), Lawton (England), Steel (Scotland), Liddell (Scotland).

'The great day has arrived, the day for football's game of games, at the world's greatest football stadium, Hampden Park,' crowed Waverley. The Rest of Europe, skippered by Johnny Carey of Manchester United and Eire, were beaten 6–1. Dr Shricker, secretary of FIFA said, 'You are still the football masters. We are still the pupils.'

Davie Meiklejohn joined the chorus: 'Our reputation the world over as the Mother Country of football remains untarnished.' But, he added sagely, 'Some day the foreigner will master the art of shooting. And when that day comes we can look out for trouble.'

We didn't have long to wait. The Hungarians electrified

Celtic goal kings: the men who scored historic goals for the Parkhead team line up – Jimmy Delaney (4,000th goal), Frank Brogan (5,000th goal), Jimmy McGrory (3,000th) and Adam McLean (2,000th goal).

soccer with victories against England in 1953 at Wembley, and against Scotland at Hampden the following year. Then in 1960 came the match that showed who were the masters now. 'ESTA MADRID!' shouted the front-page headline on 19 May 1960 and a subheading added helpfully: 'Which in anybody's language means Real Madrid won . . . 7–3.' It even elbowed aside the story that the world summit involving America's President Eisenhower, British Prime Minister Harold Macmillan and Russian leader Nikita Kruschev had broken down in Paris.

The kings of Spanish soccer had beaten Eintracht Frankfurt, who themselves had crushed Rangers in the semi-final of that season's European Cup. It was the greatest-ever European final, a spectacle which left an indelible memory on all those who saw it. Waverley summed it up:

'Never in the long and dramatic history of Hampden, Britain's greatest football stadium, have there been such scenes as marked the finish of last night's magnificent triumph by Real Madrid. The vast crowd released a tremendous roar acclaiming the winners who, after being presented with the Cup, ran round the field holding aloft the trophy to a crescendo of cheering.

'The ovation was more than appreciation of the wonder play of the Spanish team. It was a direct challenge to Scotland's football chiefs, a demonstration by the fans that they had seen something they think, justifiably, they are entitled to from our own players.'

The skill of Real Madrid stars such as Ferenc Puskas and Alfredo Di Stefano sparked off a furious debate in Scotland as to why our football lagged behind. Veteran Ian McColl, still a Rangers player but later to be appointed Scotland team manager, donned sackcloth and ashes and admitted in the *Record*: 'I felt like every Scottish footballer. We are second-raters.'

The match was refereed by the formidable Scots whistler Jack Mowat, who charged 1s 6d expenses – his train fare from his home in Burnside to nearby Hampden. Mowat retired from active refereeing after the match but for many years was the SFA's Chief Referee Supervisor.

However, beating England was still the most important task for any Scotland international squad. Two years later McColl was in charge of the Scottish side which notched the first Hampden win against England since 1937, and barefoot players went on a lap of honour. The team was Brown (Spurs), Hamilton (Dundee), Caldow (Rangers), Crerand (Celtic), McNeill (Celtic), Baxter (Rangers), Scott (Rangers), White (Spurs), St John (Liverpool), Law (Turin), Wilson (Rangers).

The key to success was the understanding between the two midfielders, Celtic's Pat Crerand and Rangers' Jim Baxter. When I interviewed Crerand for the *Record* he told me: 'We were room-mates at Kilmacolm and spent a lot of time together discussing tactics. When one of us went upfield the other stayed behind to cover the gaps. That was the lesson we learned from last year's Wembley defeat.'

The remarkable Jim Rodger, a former miner turned jour-nalist, specialised in human stories, and also produced a string of hard sports news exclusively for the *Record*. He spoke to Denis Law and the Scotland hit-man revealed he had smoked half of a 25-year-old cigar. 'The cigar has had a place of pride in my father's cigar-box for 25 years. It was smoked on the day Scotland beat England 25 years ago at Hampden. And it has been taken there every two years since waiting for a win. Now at last I've finished the cigar.'

It wasn't all gloom on the domestic scene. Celtic, for whom the seasons before Jock Stein was appointed manager were known as 'the lean years', had one shining moment. That was the 7–1 League Cup victory over Rangers in 1957.

Waverley wrote of the winners:

'They fielded a team that saw every man, from goal out, at his best, combining to provide a soccer treat the like of which is too seldom seen in these degenerate days. They were entitled to sing joyfully in their bath, and must have been conscious of the indisputable fact that they had done a lot to restore faith in the traditional style of Scottish play.'

He singled out Willie Fernie, saying: 'He has no equal in all Scotland in ball control which he employed frequently to make excursions upfield to harry Rangers.' But he slated the Ibrox team:

'I must censure every wearer of the Light Blue. But in any criticism levelled against Rangers don't for one second forget the brilliance of Celtic's football. They thoroughly deserved the margin of victory.'

The teams were *Celtic*: Beattie, Donnelly, Fallon, Fernie, Evans, Peacock, Tully, Collins, McPhail, Wilson, Mochan; and the Parkhead scorers were Wilson, a hat-trick by Billy McPhail, two from Neil Mochan and a last-minute penalty by Willie Fernie. *Rangers* lined up Niven, Shearer, Caldow, McColl, Valentine, Davis, Scott, Simpson, Murray, Baird,

History is made as Celtic skipper Bertie Peacock holds up the Scottish League Cup after their 7–1 win against Rangers in the 1957 final.

Friendly foes: the first two men to win European honours for Scottish clubs – Celtic's Jock Stein (left) and Rangers' Willie Waddell.

Hubbard, with Billy Simpson getting their solitary goal.

That was to be the last trophy Celtic won for seven years, before they defeated Dunfermline 3–2 in the 1965 Cup final, only weeks after Jock Stein took over as manager. The Stein years were laden with honours for the Parkhead club. They won 25 major trophies between 1965 and his departure in 1978. It included the European Cup, the League Championship ten times (including nine in a row), the Scottish Cup eight times and the League Cup six times.

One of the most dramatic wins was the 1970 European Cup semi-final against Leeds United, managed by Stein's friend and rival, Don Revie. Celtic won the first leg by 1–0 at Elland Road, courtesy of a George Connelly goal in 40 seconds, and after the game Stein was on one of his favourite themes in a *Record* interview:

'This game was built up as a Scotland *v.* England clash. It was more than just a European Cup game. We were really playing for Scotland. They have laughed at our football long enough down here. I'm not talking about Leeds United or Don Revie, they have respect for us. I'm talking about the critics and the commentators who have rarely given credit to Scottish football. Maybe tonight's result will stop them laughing. You can talk about all the players down here, the George Bests and everyone else, but we had men to match any of them.'

The second leg was switched from Parkhead to Hampden to accommodate the giant crowd, which smashed the attendance record for a European Cup tie, and which is now unlikely ever to be beaten. A massive 135,826 fans hailed Celtic as they swept to a 2–1 win, after Leeds had levelled the score on aggregate with a Billy Bremner goal. But strikes from John Hughes and Bobby Murdoch gave the Celts victory, and the unofficial championship of Britain.

Parkhead star Bertie Auld, stripped to the waist and clutching the ball, took up most of Page One on 16 April 1970 under a headline 'CELTIC THE GREAT: NOW FOR EUROPE'. But it didn't turn out that way, for in a sour anti-climax they lost to the Dutch side, Feyenoord of Rotterdam, in the final in Milan.

Celtic's last double-winning celebration was in 1988, their centenary year, when they captured the Scottish Cup and the League Championship. They took the Cup in a dramatic last-gasp 2–1 win against Dundee United, watched by Prime Minister Margaret Thatcher. Delighted Celtic boss Billy McNeill told the *Record*: 'For sheer determination and class this team matches the Lisbon Lions.'

A season later they retained the Scottish Cup after a 1–0

Frank McAvennie celebrates his winning goal.

victory against Rangers and Alex Cameron predicted that 'The hectic power battle between the Old Firm giants will rage even more furiously next season.' But not even a psychic medium could have predicted how the balance of power in Scottish football would tilt towards Rangers. Three managers left Celtic – Billy McNeill, Liam Brady and Lou Macari – because they couldn't halt the Ibrox trophy march. And there was a bitter wrangle for the control of Celtic, which was won eventually by the rebel shareholders led by Fergus McCann.

The Old Firm's monopoly of League titles was unshakeable between 1966 and 1980, and Celtic took the bigger slice of them. Willie Waddell had guided Kilmarnock to their only championship victory in a dramatic last-day victory over rivals Hearts in 1965, but it wasn't until 1980 that a club from outside Glasgow captured the country's main football honour.

Alex Ferguson's Aberdeen were part of the 'New Firm' along with Dundee United which shook the Old Firm domination. The Aberdonians had never known such success until Ferguson emulated Stein's earlier feats at Parkhead. Before Ferguson moved to Manchester United, the Pittodrie club had won the European Cup-Winners' Cup, three League titles, four Scottish Cups (including three in a row) and one League Cup. After their 4–1 crushing of holders Rangers in the 1982 final, Alex Cameron wrote, 'The Dons were the kind of soccer task-force the Ibrox legions would love to get behind.'

Hampden joy, as Celtic players celebrate the Parkhead club's centenary with a Scottish Cup win against Dundee United . . . a second trophy to go with the League Championship.

On the march! Men with a mission, as members of the 'Celts for Change' action group demonstrate against the Parkhead board.

We've won the League! Kilmarnock boss Willie Waddell shows his joy as he leads his men on a lap of honour after they clinch the Championship against Hearts at Tynecastle in 1985.

Our Cup: Aberdeen skipper Martin Buchan shows off the Scottish Cup to the city's Lord Provost at a civic reception, 1970.

Championship joy, as Dundee United skipper Paul Hegarty shows the fans the trophy from a balcony at Dundee's City Chambers. With Hegarty are Ralph Milne, Billy Kirkwood and Paul Sturrock.

Scoring stars John Hewitt (left) and Billy Stark with manager Alex Ferguson and the Scottish Cup after their 3–0 final win over Hearts in 1986.

Opposite: Our title: Aberdeen manager Alex Ferguson embraces skipper Willie Miller, and keeper Bobby Clark looks as if he thinks it's all a dream after the Dons clinch their first-ever Championship under Ferguson with a 5–0 victory against Hibs at Easter Road.

Scottish Cup winners, 1994!
Dundee United manager
Ivan Golac (front right) and
his victorious Tannadice
squad and back-room team
celebrate their Tennent's
Scottish Cup triumph over
Rangers at Hampden.

Departure day: outgoing
manager Graeme Souness
and Rangers chairman
David Murray face a press
conference in April 1991.

Rangers manager Graeme
Souness with three of his
major signings, Mo
Johnston, Mark Hateley
and Richard Gough.

*Serious stuff, by the looks on
the faces of Graeme Souness
and striker Mo Johnston.*

New Dundee United manager Jim McLean with his Tannadice line-up for his first full season, 1972–73. The player with the trendy '70s moustache (third left, second row) is Walter Smith, later to become Rangers' boss, and beside him is his current Ibrox assistant, Archie Knox.

Dundee United won their first (and so far only) League title in 1983. It was a tremendous achievement by their volatile manager Jim McLean, but even on the day of their triumph – when they clinched the title at rivals Dundee's Dens Park ground – he was, as always, mixing gloom with the joy. The Tannadice boss told the *Record*: 'There's no way we should be champions. We have really only 12 first-team players and they've had to sustain us for 66 matches. Our trouble has been that too many fringe players have been content to play in the reserves. Some think football owes them a living. It doesn't, not anybody.'

Eleven years later Dundee United, under charismatic new manager Ivan Golac, wrecked Rangers hopes of Scottish football's first-ever back-to-back treble, with a 1–0 Tennent's Scottish Cup final victory. Golac had chided me on the eve of the final, when the *Record* exclusively revealed he had let his players have a day at the races: 'It's not *if* we win the Cup, it's *when* we win it.'

But United's win was a rare interruption in the march of

all Scotland's major trophies to Ibrox. That was started when Graeme Souness was appointed manager of Rangers in 1986, and sparked off the most remarkable revolution in Scottish football. Not even the Godfather of Scottish managers, the eminently successful Jock Stein, had been able to achieve such a massive change. Suddenly, after decades of star players being transferred south of the border, big-name English players were coming north. The salaries at Ibrox more than matched the biggest clubs in England. As Arsenal manager George Graham said to me ruefully, 'These players haven't gone to Scotland to look at the scenery.'

England internationals Terry Butcher and Chris Woods were the first of a wave of star signings which helped Rangers put a near stranglehold on domestic honours. But the transfer that rocked Scotland was their 1989 signing of Mo Johnston from Nantes. Not only was this the club's first major signing of a Catholic since before the First World War, but Johnston, a former Celtic superstar, had been on the point of re-signing for his old club. Forests of trees were cut down to provide enough newsprint to cover the event. The *Record* devoted *ten* pages to the story the morning after the most controversial transfer in Scotland's football history was announced. Alex Cameron wrote:

> 'Sanity has come to Scottish football after more than a hundred years, or has it? As I have always promised I would say when Rangers signed a Catholic . . . *well done*! The new Rangers management have to wipe out bigotry at Ibrox and are right to do so. I have been campaigning for Rangers to break their sectarian barrier since chairman David Murray, manager Graeme Souness and Mo Johnston were either still at school or in a pram.
>
> 'I sincerely hope that Johnston signing works. There is no doubt about his playing ability. But is the signing of a former Celtic player who very nearly returned for a second stint at Parkhead provocative or thoughtless? It is probably a bit of both. But despite that, everyone in football must do his best to ensure the Johnston signing works. It would be a horrendous blow to the image of Scotland as a whole if this courageous move didn't succeed.'

The month before Johnston signed for Rangers Scotland had rejoiced in the success of their team in the World Youth

Another game, another trophy! Rangers players Gough, Ally McCoist, Stuart McCall and Alexei Mikhailichenko celebrate their 2–1 Tennent's Scottish Cup final victory over Airdrie in 1992.

Cup. The Scots were only beaten on penalties in the final by Saudi Arabia, and controversy raged about the age of the Saudi side, who looked older and more physically powerful than the Scottish players. The *Record* backed the tournament from the start, giving it invaluable publicity. And although attendances were low at the first matches, 51,674 fans turned up at the final at Hampden.

On the domestic front since the Souness appointment, and then under his successor Walter Smith, Rangers have won seven of the last eight Premier Division titles – almost as complete a monopoly as Celtic in their nine-in-a-row campaigns. However, Smith achieved more success than Souness in the most demanding arena of them all, the European Cup. Rangers reached the new-style league sections of the trophy, and finished only one point behind Marseille in their section. The French club went on to beat AC Milan in the final.

It was a competition filled with drama for the Ibrox side, no match more so than the so-called battle of Britain, when they faced English champions Leeds United in the second round for the right to move into the Champions League. Leeds skipper Gary McAllister scored in the first minute at Ibrox, stunning the 43,251 crowd from which visiting fans had been banned. Rangers striker Ally McCoist said later, 'The noise level when we went out was the loudest I've heard in all my years at Ibrox. And a minute later, when they scored, it was the quietest.'

But an own-goal by Leeds keeper John Lukic and another strike by McCoist gave Rangers a 2–1 aggregate lead. At Elland Road, with only a handful of Ibrox supporters managing to beat the fan ban, it was Rangers' turn to stun Leeds early on. Mark Hateley scored in the second minute and McCoist in 58 minutes to put Rangers 4–1 ahead on aggregate. Eric Cantona, in one of his last appearances for Leeds before he moved to Manchester United, pulled a goal back, but it was never going to stop the progress of Smith's men.

Hateley, unknowingly echoing Jock Stein at the same ground 23 years earlier, said, 'It's wonderful after being written off by so many people down south.' One of the main Rangers heroes was Andy Goram who said, 'I hope this ends once and for all the jokes in England about Scottish keepers.' The next day I reported how Ally McCoist had been mobbed when he appeared for an autograph-signing session at a sports shop in Argyle Street, Glasgow. Whatever else has changed, Scotland's passion for big-time football remains undiminished.

Just champion! It's 1993, and Rangers celebrate another title triumph.

Hall of Fame

From Snooker to Swimming,
Cycling to Grand Prix

Jim Clark

Some experts believe Jim Clark, Scotland's first World Champion racing-driver, was the greatest driver ever. The modest Scotsman from the Borders won the title in 1963 and took it again two years later. In 1964 he captured the Indianapolis 500 race – the first non-American to clinch such a victory in 49 years. The amazed Yanks voted him Professional Athlete of the Year.

But always in their chosen sport there is constant worry for the driver's loved ones. After Clark's victory in the Italian Grand Prix to clinch his first title his mother gave a remarkable interview to the *Record*'s Ellen Grehan. The story, written in September 1963, no doubt has the same message more than 30 years later – especially in 1994 when Grand Prix racing mourned the deaths of more top drivers.

'If Jim only knew how much I worried about him he would give up racing. I shall never ask him to do it, however. It's in his blood, it's his life now. All I can do is wait and pray and hope that after a season as World Champion he'll get over this craze for speed.

'For several nights before he takes part in a race I pray nothing will happen to him or any of the boys.

Opposite: World Champion motor racing star Jim Clark, draped in laurel leaves and surrounded by trophies.

Before he leaves I say to him, "Now, Jim, be careful and don't take any risks." He laughs and says, "Don't worry, Mum. I'll be okay." On the night of a race I go upstairs till it's over and he phones me to say that everything's fine. Jim hates me to say this and I know he'll be furious when he reads it. But I hope he retires soon – I really do.'

Five years later, on Monday, 8 April 1968, the *Record*'s front-page story started with the grim news:

'Jim Clark, the "Flying Scotsman" of the racing track, died in a mystery, somersaulting crash on Germany's Hockenheim circuit yesterday.

'Clark, 32, World Champion driver in 1963 and 1965, was driving a Formula II Lotus-Ford in a race for the German national trophy. He had roared away to a perfect start on a track which was wet and slippery.

'Then, on the fifth lap, when he was lying eighth, Clark, who earned £60,000 a year as Britain's top driver, lost control at 170 mph on a sweeping curve. Eye-witnesses said the rear of the car seemed to break up. It slipped away to the right then disappeared over the rim of the track, turning over and over. Seconds later it smashed broadside-on into a tree.

'Clark's team-mate Graham Hill, who has raced with him all over the world, was also taking part in the race. He telephoned Clark's parents in Berwickshire with news of the tragedy. Last night Jim's father, Mr James Clark, said: "Racing was his life. We had to accept it and were proud of him. Now it has ended."'

Four days later, on Thursday, 11 April, the *Record*'s report by Bill Robertson of the funeral began:

'It was a 1937 Rolls-Royce, shimmering in the spring sunshine, that carried Jim Clark on his last five-miles-per-hour drive. It took him on the last leg of the journey from the Hockenheim circuit in Germany to the village of Chirnside in Berwickshire. The kirk bell tolled a slow, slow peal, scattering the sparrows nesting in the tower. The pipe organ blared its mournful message.

'They buried him in a corner of the ancient churchyard in a plot overlooking the rolling rich acres of Berwickshire, the county he loved. The final resting-place of the quiet Scot who followed Moss, Nuvolari, Ascari, Fangio. And proved greater than any of them.'

One motor racing legend salutes another: three-times World Champion Jackie Stewart with the Jim Clark memorial trophy he was awarded in 1974.

Jackie Stewart

A year after Jim Clark's death another Scot became the king of Grand Prix racing. And, accompanied by the flourish of his signature, Jackie Stewart told the *Record* exclusively of his coronation.

'Yesterday at 4.42 p.m. I achieved my life's ambition by winning the World Championship the way I wanted to, with a convincing victory. I could have taken the title simply by coasting home in the Italian Grand Prix at Monza. Second, third or even fourth place would have given me enough points. But from start to finish taking first place was all that mattered. If I set out to win I go all the way. Second-rate victories are not for me. Taking the chequered flag after 68 laps of tough racing and after eight Grand Prix events was the climax of my career – but it doesn't mean I'll be calling it a day.

'When I sit back and try to call my feelings to order, I think of the days when it all started: the racing days of my brother Jimmy when I got the fever; the Charterhall days, leaving the house very early in the morning to drive down to the track under the nom-de-plume of A.N. Other so that my mother would not find out and be upset; the excitement when I was asked by David Murray

Family dynasty: former World Champion Jackie Stewart with his son, Paul, also a racing driver, 1993.

to drive for Ecurie Ecosse, breaking a lap record at Charterhall in the team's Cooper Monaco.'

He paid a tribute to Jim Clark:

'I admired him more than any other driver, and was very proud to be his friend. Jim was terrific. I always looked up to him, and even although he died on the track, I would never rate myself above him in any way.'

But by 1973 Stewart, who had won two more world titles, had had enough. Malcolm McDougall reported: 'Triple World Champion Jackie Stewart yesterday abdicated as king of the track – for family reasons.' And 18 years later, when his son, Paul, became a racing driver, Stewart confessed:

'I don't like it. If he had been a golfer or a tennis player I'd have been much happier. It's purely because of the dangers of racing. The lifestyle I have enjoyed has been absolutely wonderful. But, as a father concerned about his son I only remember the dangers. I admit that is very selfish, when I had so much pleasure from my racing career. It is, of course, not as dangerous a sport as when I started out. But it's still not Nick Faldo hitting golf balls.'

David Wilkie

The telegram said it all: 'From Scotland's number-one paper – and our two million readers – to superstar David Wilkie. You're Scotland's golden boy.'

Tall, tanned and only 22, Wilkie reached the pinnacle of his fame at the 1976 Olympic Games in Montreal, when he won gold in the 200 metres freestyle swimming, and silver in the 100 metres. The paper detailed his life story:

'He was born in Ceylon, where his father was boss of an export business. When he was 11 he came to Scotland, as a boarder at Edinburgh's Daniel Stewart's College. He joined the Warrender Club where he quickly caught the attention of two coaches, Frank Thomas, a former Scottish international swimmer, and PT teacher John Ashton. They encouraged him to take up competitive swimming.

'Frank said: "He was a terrific worker when you could get him into the water. But he had great difficulty in disciplining himself when it came to training. But getting *him* to recognise it and come to training regularly

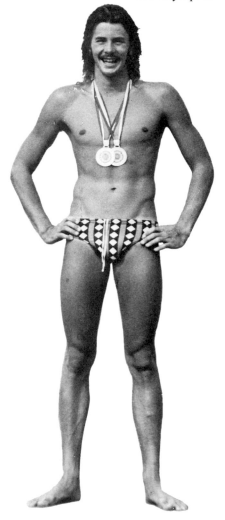

Medallion man: swimmer David Wilkie with the gold and silver medals he won at the Olympics.

Wilkie and the water babes: Olympic star David Wilkie meets schoolkids at a fundraising event in Glasgow.

was a different matter. He just could not or would not get up in the morning. I gave him an alarm clock as a present. But even that didn't help."

'But it all came right for David, who was a student at Miami University at the time of his victory. He said: "I got a huge lump in my throat when they played *God Save the Queen*. It is a wonderful feeling to finish first in the Olympics, and to go out of swimming right at the top. I have lived for this moment for four years. Now I'd like to make Scotland my home."'

In 1964 at the Tokyo Olympics, Bobby McGregor won a silver medal, finishing second to American Don Schollander in the 100 metres. The Falkirk-born swimmer, who suffered his first spring defeat in two years according to the *Record*, summed up the race succinctly: 'I had a good start and a good turn. I gave all I got. It wasn't enough, the stronger man in a finish won.'

Winnie Shaw

Scottish tennis players who become a success away from their own country are as rare as baseball players plying their trade outside the United States. But Winnie Shaw was one of those very few. If she didn't reach the very top she at least scaled the heights.

Her mother, Winnie Mason, was twice Scottish tennis

The King and Queen of Scottish sport: Jim Clark and Winnie Shaw with their Usher Vaux Sportsman and Sportswoman awards for 1965.

Opposite: Winnie Shaw at Wimbledon, showing her skills at the mecca of world tennis.

champion, and her father, Angus Shaw, was one of Glasgow's most noted journalists, with spells as news editor of the *Evening News*, the *Sunday Mail* and the *Evening Times*. Her grandfather, Sir David Mason, was the Lord Provost of Glasgow whose name is on the plaque inside Ibrox as the man who opened the impressive main stand of the ground in 1929.

Winnie reached the quarter-finals of Wimbledon in two successive years, 1971 and 1972. The *Record* said on 30 June 1970:

'Scotland's Winnie Shaw was unceremoniously ushered out of the women's singles at Wimbledon yesterday. The 23-year-old Clarkston girl, who had been Britain's last hope for the women's title, crashed 6–2, 6–0 to Rosemary Casals of America. It was Winnie's biggest defeat for some time and she said afterwards: "Rosemary never gave me a chance to settle down. I guess I was a bit nervous."'

A year later she lost 6–2, 6–1 to Australian Margaret Court. She said later, 'I wanted more than anything to win Wimbledon. I have failed in my bid but I don't think there is any disgrace to lose to such a champion as Margaret Court.'

Winnie went on to reach the women's doubles that year with fellow-Scot Joyce Williams. She twice contested the Australian semi-finals and was beaten in the final of the women's doubles and the mixed doubles at the French Championships.

I liked best the story of when she played in a Federation Cup match in Athens and the Greek umpire twice introduced her as 'Shaw, representing England'. She told him politely but firmly: 'I'm Scottish and I'm representing Great Britain, not England.'

She also played international golf for Scotland. Winnie married tennis star Keith Wooldridge and sadly died of cancer in 1992, aged 45.

Freuchie

I haven't checked every copy, but I don't suppose the *Daily Record* has ever led Page One with a Scottish cricketing story – until Monday, 2 September 1985. The headlines blazed out: 'SUPER SCOTS BOWL THEM OVER'. And the men who achieved this incredible feat? Well, read on:

'Fabulous Freuchie yesterday batted the English into submission. They defeated the Auld Enemy at their own game to take the National Village Cricket Championship – and they did it at the home of cricket, Lords. Dave Christie, 48, captained his team to a nail-biting victory over Rowledge from stockbroker-belt Surrey.

'And last night double celebrations were under way. Seven hundred villagers, almost half Freuchie's 1,746 population, were whooping it up in London and the rest celebrating back home in Fife. One said, "I have never known anything like this." And Dave Christie, promising a party in the clubhouse tonight, said, "The whole village will be there."'

James Laing had reported on the build-up:
'The village of Freuchie, as bonny a hamlet as can be found in the confines of Fife, lies a few miles north of Glenrothes. It's my pleasure to report that the people of the place have gone gloriously mad.

'The centre of this phenomenon is the local cricket club, a low white building with a better-than-adequate bar and a view over the tiny green pitch where members play that very English game. And they have played so well they have beaten all-comers from an entry of 639 sides scattered the length and breadth of Britain to reach the final of the National Village Cricket Championship. They are going to Lords, mecca of world cricket.'

Colin Dunne described the scene at the hallowed HQ of world cricket:
'The men from Freuchie could have crept quietly into the famous old ground, muttered a few courtesies about who won or lost, and slipped discreetly away. Instead, they did it the way the Scots know best, with high hearts, kilts swinging and behind blazing bagpipes. Imagine Vera Lynn arriving at Braemar for the caber-tossing and you have some idea of the glorious impudence of the scene.
'To the specially-composed Freuchie's *March To Lords*, Pipe-Major Alistair Pirnie led the team through the Grace Gates (after W.G. of course), cheered all the way by their 700 or so supporters.

'The finish was dramatic. Both teams had scored 134. Their opponents had been all out and Freuchie still had two batsmen left. That made them the winners and

Stewart Irvine was named man of the match for his big hitting.

'Who were the other team? Oh, they were from Surrey or somewhere like that. What would they know about cricket?'

Stephen Hendry

Snooker star Stephen Hendry is the most successful Scottish sportsman in this or any other century. He has won four world titles, and swollen his bank balance with career winnings of an amazing £3.5 million. His manager Ian Doyle sometimes complains Stephen doesn't get enough credit in Scotland for his achievements. I hope he excludes the *Daily Record* from his criticisms. The cuttings files on Hendry in the *Record* library occupy an entire shelf of a massive cabinet, and sportswriter John Docherty has followed Hendry along each step of his triumphal way. Here he is in January 1987, quoting Englishman Danny Fowler at the Mercantile Classic in Blackpool before playing 17-year-old Hendry: 'I don't know what the fuss is all about. Stephen is just another player as far as I'm concerned.' Mr Fowler was soon to find out differently as he exited stage left from the tournament, and the world of snooker was blitzed by the new prodigy.

He claimed his first crown at the famous Crucible Theatre in Sheffield in April 1990 – and took over most of Page One. 'STEPHEN'S £2m KISS' was the headline on a story which read:

'Scotland's wonderboy Stephen Hendry was crowned king of world snooker last night. The cool kid from South Queensferry lifted the world title in Sheffield as the whole country cheered in front of their tellies.

'And rushing to congratulate him was girlfriend Mandy Tart, who was right on cue with a big kiss . . . a £2 million smacker to be precise. That is how much super Stephen will pocket as World Champ over the next year *in addition* to the £120,000 official prize purse. And that puts Britain's other superstars such as US Masters golf champ Nick Faldo and race ace Nigel Mansell in the cash shade.'

He was the youngest-ever champion. Docherty wrote: 'Snooker's new king Stephen Hendry last night delivered

That old championship feeling: snooker star Stephen Hendry holds up the Embassy World Championship trophy after successfully defending his title, 1994.

The prizes of success: Stephen Hendry and girlfriend Mandy Tart with his £180,000 Bentley Continental and the Embassy World Championship trophy.

Champion and challenger: Stephen Hendry and Jimmy White, the Londoner he has defeated four times for the Embassy World title.

his rivals a chilling warning. "I want to be the Steve Davis of the 1990s," rapped the ice-cool tartan sensation. Hendry's fabulous 18–12 Embassy World Championship victory over Jimmy White has made him hungry for even more success. "I'm going to have a real crack at winning more titles than Davis. Steve dominated snooker in the 1980s. That's what I plan to do in the 1990s."

'Hendry braced himself for the challenge ahead: "Now that I'm number one, I'm the top target for everyone. But I don't feel under any extra pressure. I just want to enjoy playing, and hopefully win as many titles as I can."'

He's done that all right, reeling off victories in '92, '93 and '94 – and all of them against the luckless Jimmy White. But, for sheer guts, the latest title win surely dwarfs the others. He played with a broken left arm, suffered at the start of the Embassy title bid when he slipped in the bathroom of his hotel. His extra reward for winning was a Bentley from his manager. His friend, John Docherty, told the story:

'Snooker king Stephen Hendry climbed into his sparkling new £180,000 Bentley yesterday ... and said the two-and-a-half-ton dream-machine would be going straight into the garage. "It's a bit flash," smiled Hendry, just 12 hours after his spellbinding 18–17 World Championship triumph against Jimmy White.

'Stephen was quick to acknowledge the magic of White. "Jimmy has always been my idol. I love watching him more than anyone else. I knew that every man and his dog wanted Jimmy to win the title, and I hope he will one day – but not against me."'

Alex Cameron, praising Hendry's sportsmanship, said: 'He sets an example every youngster should copy. Humility is still his trademark. Prima donna footballers, rope-jumping boxers and club-throwing golfers can all learn from him.

'How many of them *would* refuse an advantage offered by a referee? In my experience *none*. Yet Hendry did, despite the fact he was performing in front of a hostile English audience. He was poised to lead 17–15 when referee John Williams awarded him a free ball after White failed to beat a snooker. "Are you sure?" queried Hendry. Williams had a second look and overruled himself. This was like Richard Gough or Paul McStay refusing a penalty. White swooped on the reprieve, snookered honest Hendry and cleared up to win on the black.

'It was typical of Hendry, unfailingly unassuming, never boastful and a man who lets his talent with the cue do the talking. Coaches in *every* sport should show Hendry in action, and see there's still a place for Corinthians.'

Dick McTaggart

The pinnacle of Dick McTaggart's career was in the 1956 Olympic Games in Melbourne, when he won the only boxing gold medal ever captured by a Scot. He had an incredible 634 fights in his amateur career, but that first Monday in December was his greatest. Peter Wilson, rated Britain's finest boxing writer, enthused in the *Record* of Monday, 3 December 1956, in the purple prose he adored:

'In this colourful West Melbourne Stadium where the flags of a score of nations had fluttered so bravely under the red and blue and amber stage-lights shining from the roof, Dick McTaggart, the sometime Dundee butcher, currently a cook with the RAF, who celebrated his 21st birthday just before leaving for this trip, was getting the supreme honour. Shyly, the young Scottish lightweight with the blond scrubbing-brush haircut stood clasping the gigantic Val Barker Cup which had been presented to him as "the most efficient amateur boxer in the Games".

'The trophy, which perpetuates the name of the old ABA champion who before his death was secretary of the international ABA, is in fact a token whereby a man can honestly call himself the amateur champion of champions of the whole world. And this is the first time it had ever come to Britain.

'McTaggart, one our six southpaws, had clinched his right to it by the way he dealt with Hans Kurschat, the powerful German holder of the European lightweight title. In the first round the Scot dropped Kurschat twice with his right, which is deceptively and incredibly powerful for a southpaw. McTaggart went on to win the next two rounds as well, punching so accurately that he looked as though he could thread a needle with his boxing gloves. And although he tired in the last minute of the last two sessions, he was a clear and worthy winner.

'The McTaggarts are not a family to be trifled with. In 1954 when Dick won the RAF title, his brother Peter won the Navy title. And yet again another brother won the Middle East Army crown.

'Yet ironically McTaggart thought of giving up boxing some 18 months ago until Jack Roy, our trainer here, persuaded him to soldier on with it.'

McTaggart, nicknamed Dandy Dick, won bronze in the 1960 Olympics in Rome and completed his gold collection with titles in the European Championships and the Empire Games. He later became coach to Scotland's amateur boxing team.

It's December 1956, and Dick McTaggart brings home the perfect Christmas present from Melbourne – the Val Barker trophy as the best boxer in the Olympics to go with his Olympic gold medal.

Graeme Obree

Few outside his immediate family and a handful of cycling supporters had heard of 27-year-old Graeme Obree before the summer of 1993. But by the following December he had been voted BBC Scotland's Sports Personality of the Year, and, in accepting a similar award from the Sports Photographers' Association, won over a hard-bitten media audience with an after-lunch speech.

The man and his machine which took him to glory: World Champion Graeme Obree with his revolutionary bike.

A bicycle built for two Scottish champions: cyclist Graeme Obree and snooker star Stephen Hendry.

A punch of triumph: Scots jockey Willie Carson shows his joy at yet another winner.

Obree pedalled to fame in July 1993 on a machine that was hand-made, and John Docherty reporting his amazing rise:

'Obree scorched into the history books when he covered almost 33 miles in 60 memorable minutes at the Hamar Velodrome in Oslo. That beat the previous record by more than a quarter of a mile – and he did it on a home-built bike which literally cost washers.

'Now cycling's superstars are chasing his new one-hour world best with Olympic 400 metres pursuit king Chris Boardman the first to have a crack at it in Bordeaux on Friday. "Everyone is out to get me," said Obree at his Ayr home. "I'm the guy they're all gunning for and I don't mind a bit."

'Obree, married with a 15-month-old son, Ewan, is a one-off. Lack of money has always been a problem – he has even had his phone cut off. The development of Boardman's revolutionary bike cost millions of pounds. But Obree, armed only with his imagination and a few tools, built his own flying machine for around £100 – give or take a few nuts and bolts! "I spent four months building the bike at the Irvine Cycles shop," said Obree. "Basically I had a plan in my head and got stuck into the job. Thankfully, it has all turned out very well." Obree, who has all the makings of an inventor, even used parts from an old washing-machine. "I used any bits and pieces I could get my hands on," he said.'

A month later he became the first Briton for 35 years to win the world 4,000 metres pursuit crown when he outclassed Frenchman Phillipe Ermenault by nearly three seconds. He also smashed his own world record by just under two seconds. He is a home-spun hero, more used to the accolades of the fans and sporting press on the Continent where cycling is rated one of the top sports. Obree is the star that Europe fêted and Scotland, slightly to its surprise, I suspect, found on its own doorstep.

Willie Carson

When jockey Willie Carson is interviewed the Scottish links are hard to hear. Yet the man who has ridden three Derby winners started life in Stirling in 1943. The galloping Grandad has returned more than 3,500 winners in his 35 competitive years in the saddle, including 17 Classic races. As the *Record* said: 'Not bad for a 51-year-old former paper boy from Stirling', and as the rider himself said after he won the 1994 Derby on Erhaab: 'Grandad did well.' In a profile after that victory the *Record* said:

'Scotland's most successful jockey has a past as chequered as his riding-shirts. Two brushes with death, a fall-out with the Queen, a bust-up with his sons and disputes over his racing tactics have made Carson a hero and a villain.

'In 1981 Carson suffered his most serious injury after a death-defying fall from Silent Knot. He was hospitalised for months with a fractured skull, broken vertebrae and a snapped wrist, completing a total of 36 broken bones over a career spanning five decades. And splitting headaches are a painful reminder of his accident that often turn the chirpy, cheeky Carson into a snappy chappy.

'He's a self-made millionaire, living on a 150-acre Gloucestershire stud farm – a far cry from the two-bedroom council flat he was brought up in. Carson's outspoken attitude has got him into hot water. And last year the publication of his autobiography, *Up Front*, angered his own sons whom he branded "stupid".

'Punters have a love-hate relationship with Carson. But the vast majority have certainly had a few beers over the years, courtesy of the Flying Scot. Even to those who don't follow racing Willie will always be remembered for his hyena-like laugh on the BBC TV quiz, *A Question of Sport*.'

Richard Corsie

Bowls has always suffered from the tag of an old man's sport. Not true now – if indeed it ever was – and Richard Corsie, at only 27, has proved the perfect ambassador for the TV age. The sport now receives massive coverage, and Corsie has been its main star, with three World Indoor titles in six years. The first time he did it the *Record* reported:

'Postman Richard Corsie took delivery of the world indoor crown yesterday in first-class style. He sent fellow-Scot Wood tumbling to a 5–0 whitewash in yesterday's final at Preston. It was a brilliant display by the

22-year-old from Edinburgh, who takes over the mantle of World Champion from countryman Hugh Duff. And it left the luckless Wood with second prize yet again.

'Corsie, who continued to keep the pressure on, added the fourth set 7–3 and said: "I knew then that the title was within my grasp. And I just had to keep cool before the evening session began." That session, in fact, was over in just 19 minutes for Corsie to complete a 7–2, 7–5, 7–6, 7–3, 7–0 win.'

When he won in 1993 he revealed his love of another game: 'I'm dying for a game of golf,' said Corsie after he had beaten fellow-Scot Jim McCann of Blantyre. Richard revealed: 'I took up golf a couple of months ago and I'm really enjoying it. I find it very relaxing.' Not many of us would agree with that assessment, but he's obviously got a natural eye and the defeated McCann said, 'He's a great

A switch of sports for bowls champion Richard Corsie when he met the Scottish junior curling team of Alan McDougall, James Dryburgh, Fraser McGregor and Colin Beckett.

player with all the shots. I don't care if I never win another game. I've had a wonderful time in Preston and enjoyed every minute of it.'

Former Rangers footballer Bob Sutherland enjoyed his moment of glory in 1983, and John Docherty reported:

'The smiling, 40-year-old Scot shot his way into a runaway 21–10 victory over Canadian Burnie Gill in the final of the Embassy World Indoor Championship at Coatbridge. "This is the happiest day in my life. It's magic," enthused sales rep Bob, from Livingston, who picked up £4,500 for his week's work.

Amazingly Bob only took up bowls in 1964 after a knee injury cut short his career at Ibrox. "I was with Rangers at the same time as John Greig and Ronnie McKinnon. But now that I'm world champion I'm pleased I turned to bowls."'

Taking on the World

Football's World Cup Adventures

Scotland's World Cup record reflects the roller-coaster of the nation's sporting fortunes. The ups have produced some of the greatest moments of ecstasy in our football history, the downs some of the most bitter disappointments. And through all the campaigns there has been one thread linking the failure of the first trip to the finals, in Switzerland in 1954, to another flop when the Scots missed out on the 1994 finals in America. The team's fortunes are always intertwined with the man in charge, the team manager. From Andy Beattie in 1954 to Andy Roxburgh in the last World Cup campaign, all have been at the centre of major controversies during their spells in office.

The pre-war World Cups passed Scotland by, and the other home countries as well, as the British representatives had resigned from the world football governing authority, FIFA. The British football associations rejoined FIFA in 1947, and for the first World Cup contest after that – the 1950 finals in Brazil – the Home International Championship, then the peak representative honour as far as British football was concerned, was to be a qualifying section. FIFA generously decreed that

Opposite: Scotland keeper Jimmy Cowan gathers the ball under the wary eye of skipper George Young in a 1948 game against Belgium at Hampden.

65

the top two nations from the group could travel to Brazil. The SFA arrogantly snubbed them by saying Scotland would only go as British champions. After failing to beat England at Hampden we finished runners-up and stayed at home.

It is fascinating to observe the changing attitudes in sport as well as society: if the SFA were offered such a deal for the 1998 finals in France they would lock the door until the agreement was signed in triplicate. Alas, such procedures are no longer on the table. But they were for the 1954 finals in Switzerland, and this time the SFA agreed Scotland would compete, whether they finished as champions or runners-up in the Home International Championship. Scotland were runners-up and accepted the invitation to play in Switzerland. But the old antipathy to the World Cup had not been totally swept away. The belief that we should build a Hadrian's Wall to protect ourselves from the dreaded 'foreigners' was typified by the *Record*'s chief football writer, Waverley. In his message on his departure to Switzerland he wrote:

'I have repeatedly said I am among those who hold the view that we should *not* have entered the World Cup; circumstances which surround our soccer make-up see us under a big handicap against the foreigners who have country, not club, as their first consideration.'

The first of them all: Scotland team manager Andy Beattie (centre) talks to SFA secretary Willie Allan, as selector Willie Dunn (left) has a look at his menu.

This only echoed in June a similar sentiment put forward in February at an SFA Council meeting by Rangers director George Brown, a former Scotland captain. 'The basis of national football in Scotland is club football. It is folly to imitate the Continentals and produce 11 robots.' This was only a few months after the fabulous Hungarian side, 'The Magical Magyars', had trounced England 6–3 at Wembley. Mr Brown was unimpressed: 'Hungary is not the world's leading football country as some people would have us believe. The leading football country is Britain, because the game was built here on club football.' Waverley described this nonsense as one of the finest speeches made in recent years in the SFA chamber.

The same issue, 2 February 1954, also included the news that Scotland had appointed our first-ever international team manager. Significantly it was not the main item on the page.

In fact, he wasn't even given the title of team manager, but was dubbed 'official in charge'. Huddersfield Town manager Andy Beattie was the man who made history. He was a former Preston and Scotland full-back and his job was part-time, with the team still being picked by the SFA selection committee. He wasn't too forthcoming about his new post, only saying in the slightly stilted language of the time: 'I cannot in the meantime make any comment. But you can be assured that whatever the

This line-up beat Ireland 1–0 at Hampden, 1957. Back row (left to right): Parker (Falkirk), McColl (Rangers), Younger (Liverpool), Hewie (Charlton), Cowie (Dundee). Front row: Scott (Rangers), Mudie (Blackpool), Reilly (Hibs), Young (Rangers), Collins (Celtic), Fernie (Celtic).

The 1958 line-up against Wales: left to right: Bobby Collins (Celtic), Eric Caldow (Rangers), John Hewie (Charlton), Tommy Younger (Liverpool), Jackie Mudie (Blackpool), Alex Parker (Falkirk), Alex Scott (Rangers), Ian Gardiner (Motherwell), Tommy Ewing (Partick Thistle), Tommy Docherty (Preston), Willie Fernie (Celtic), Bobby Evans (Celtic), trainer Dawson Walker.

task ahead I'll approach it conscientiously.'

The SFA didn't regard the World Cup as anything special. Only 13 players were in the travelling party for Switzerland, and although Rangers provided the backbone of the Scotland side at that time no Ibrox players were included, as the club were on a close-season goodwill tour of North America. The unlucky 13 who went to Switzerland were Fred Martin (Aberdeen), Willie Cunningham (Preston), Jock Aird (Burnley), Bobby Evans (Celtic), Tommy Docherty (Preston), Doug Cowie (Dundee), Jimmy Davidson (Partick Thistle), Johnny McKenzie (Partick Thistle), Willie Ormond (Hibs), George Hamilton (Aberdeen), Allan Brown (Blackpool), Neil Mochan (Celtic), Willie Fernie (Celtic).

The players even had to take their own club training gear and Waverley gloomily assessed Scotland's chances in a section which included Austria and holders Uruguay: 'It's the first time I have made a trip abroad lacking optimism.' Cheerfulness was never one of the writer's characteristics, though he did manage a 'where there's life there's hope' line. If

he had only known that World Cup life was soon to end he would have been even more pessimistic.

Scotland lost the opening game in Zurich by 1–0 to Austria but the paper reported:

'Our boys went down with a St Andrews Cross firmly nailed to the mast. No team could have fought harder. For so long I have been given cause to criticise the Scotland team. It is a positive pleasure now to give them high praise. I now look forward to our game with Uruguay with more hope than I have held since first I knew we were to compete in the global tournament.'

Sadly for Waverley's optimism, his hopes were cruelly crushed, but not before an eve-of-the-match sensation when team boss Beattie announced he was quitting. In a memorable exclusive, Waverley's story was splashed across Page One with Beattie saying: 'Tomorrow after we meet Uruguay – win, lose or draw – I'm going home.' The writer saw sinister reasons for the manager's resignation:

'He told me the reason for relinquishing the appointment is that he spends too much time away from his home, wife and children. I said: "I don't believe you, Andy, there are other reasons." He became poker-faced in response. I had known for some time there has been a difference between the policy, adopted by certain misguided officials of the SFA and Andrew Beattie.'

By the following afternoon Beattie must have wished he had left before the game, as the helpless Scots were trounced 7–0 by the defending champions of Uruguay. The first of a depressing series of inquests on Scotland's World Cup failures had started. 'We can't lace their boots now,' said Waverley, working himself into a fine old lather. 'We have been content to live in the mud-hut of soccer while the South Americans have been building marble palaces. There was not one redeeming feature from which I could take a penny's-worth of consolation.'

The Scotland squad arrived back to be greeted with a Page One headline: 'THE LOT-TO-LEARN TEAM COMES HOME AGAIN'. And on the back page there was a picture of the crestfallen Scotland keeper, Fred Martin, who had seen those seven Uruguayan goals fly past him. Beattie did return for another short spell as Scotland manager, but it didn't include any more World Cup matches. He must have thought he had

Scotland's Jock Aird is beaten to the ball by Luis Cruz of Uruguay in the 1954 World Cup, and the South Americans went on to win the match 7–0.

suffered enough.

For the 1958 finals in Sweden the Scots had to qualify for the first time against Continental opposition, and they finished ahead of Spain and Switzerland in a three-nation group. A Hampden crowd saw a memorable 4–2 win against a star-studded Spanish team which included Suarez, Di Stefano and Gento. It's the only time I ever heard reporters in the Hampden press-box hammer their desks in appreciation of a Scotland performance.

This time there was no team manager. Manchester United boss Matt Busby had agreed to take charge of the Scotland squad in Sweden, but the dreadful, tragic Munich air disaster changed all that. His injuries in the crash which killed so many of the Busby Babes proved too severe and he pulled out of the World Cup, depriving not only Scotland but also the world's premier football tournament of the one chance of Busby measuring his managerial skills at the very top level.

Some things never change. Many thousands of words have been spilt over the decades reporting the battles between the TV companies and the SFA over live football, and 1958 was no exception. The *Record*'s sports editor James Cameron had coined the memorable headline 'NOT ON YOUR TELLY!', and it was trotted out in June of that year, just as it has been every year since then. This time, the SFA ruled there would be no live screening of mid-week World Cup matches in Scotland until the semi-finals. Officials of junior football had objected, and the SFA sustained their appeal. The ban was eventually lifted, but not before the SFA uttered dark threats to the TV companies about future negotiations being jeopardised because they had insisted on screening games.

The Scotland squad had trainer Dawson Walker of Clyde in charge, but the team was still picked by the SFA selection committee, who had also enlarged the party to 22 players.

Waverley was happier this time: 'I have the feeling I may be sending you happy messages from Scandinavia.' And after the opening game against Yugoslavia, a 1–1 draw with a goal by Jimmy Murray of Hearts, he reported: 'I have just left a small colony of Scots now wildly cheering our fighting team and joining in the applause of a thousand Swedes who had been rooting for us. Let there be no taking away from the credit of tonight's achievement.'

But trouble was brewing. There was a fall-out between

the SFA officials and the press, not an unusual event in the hot-house atmosphere of World Cup finals, and Waverley complained:

'The Scottish journalists among the 1,200 newspapermen from all over the globe are the only ones not given any official statements by the representatives of their own country. Perhaps my profession is not popular with the little group of gentlemen in possession of temporary authority. Well, well. I have seen a lot of their kind come and go.'

Then the tournament followed a familiar downhill slide by Scotland. Despite goals by Blackpool's Jackie Mudie and Bobby Collins of Celtic, Scotland were defeated 3–2 by Paraguay, the paper claiming that 'Scotland lost a game which they should have won before the half-time whistle'.

That was followed by a 2–1 defeat by France (Sammy Baird of Rangers scoring Scotland's goal), and the *Record* said: 'We cannot complain of the final blow that put us on the global boxing canvas.'

The type on 'The Guilty Men of Scottish Football' was dusted down yet again. 'I blame selectors,' said Waverley and the next day followed up with 'I blame the players', accusing them of staying up too late and eating too many cream cakes.

The Scotland line-up of 1961: Back row (left to right): manager Ian McColl, Duncan MacKay (Celtic), Dave Mackay (Spurs), Jackie Plenderleith (Man City), Lawrie Leslie (Airdrie), Jim Baxter (Rangers), Eric Caldow (Rangers), Jimmy Millar (Rangers), trainer Dawson Walker. Front row: George Herd (Clyde), Denis Law (Man City), Alex Young (Hearts), Ralph Brand (Rangers), Davy Wilson (Rangers).

Davy Wilson congratulates his Ibrox team-mate Ian McColl (left), the new Scotland team boss.

Flare-up in a 1962 game against Uruguay at Hampden as Davy Wilson restrains team-mate Pat Crerand.

But there would be no chance for 16 long years for any Scottish player to stay up too late or eat too much at the next three World Cup finals. The lean years had arrived.

For the 1962 finals the SFA again appointed a manager, choosing Ian McColl although he was still a Rangers player at the time, and the selection committee made sure they retained the right to pick the team. The target this time was Chile, and again the Scots were in a three-nation qualifying group, along with Czechoslovakia and the Republic of Ireland. The Scots lost 4–0 in Czechoslovakia, Celtic's Pat Crerand being sent off, but they saved their qualifying chances with a memorable 3–2 defeat of the Czechs at Hampden thanks to two goals by Denis Law and one by Ian St John.

I remember that game well. It was the first time I had my name on a front-page story in the *Record* as I reported the morning after the game on 26 September 1961: 'This was the day the Hampden roar was re-born.' It was a Scotland team which had class stamped all through it, comprising: Brown (Spurs), MacKay (Celtic), Caldow (Rangers), Crerand (Celtic), McNeill (Celtic), Baxter (Rangers), Scott (Rangers), White (Spurs), St John (Liverpool), Law (Torino), Wilson (Rangers). Surely one of Scotland's many football regrets is that this team never made it to the World Cup finals. They did, however, force a play-off against the Czechs in Brussels and took the lead twice with goals by St John, but eventually lost 4–2 in extra time. The only consolation was that Czechoslovakia proved their worth by going on to lose in the final to Brazil.

By the next campaign, time had run out for Ian McColl. He was sacked in a late-night meeting with SFA Secretary Willie Allan while the team were preparing at Largs for two matches against Poland and Finland. McColl's wife, Jessie, rushed to his defence and Page One was cleared for the departure of yet another Scottish international manager: 'I'm absolutely disgusted with the whole business,' she said.

Celtic manager, Jock Stein, just starting his legendary span as Parkhead boss, took over as part-time international chief. But even he couldn't avert a major disaster against Poland at Hampden. Scotland lost 2–1 despite an early goal by Celtic skipper Billy McNeill, but a stunning double by the Poles in the last five minutes was too much for Stein's men. Waverley was scathing: 'I have seen, home and abroad, many

They're going to face Italy in the World Cup, and the tension shows. Back row (left to right): John Greig (Rangers), Davie Provan (Rangers), Bill Brown (Spurs), Bobby Murdoch (Celtic), Jim Baxter (Sunderland), Ronnie McKinnon (Rangers). Front row: Neil Martin (Sunderland), Billy Bremner (Leeds), Willie Johnston (Rangers), John Hughes (Celtic), Willie Henderson (Rangers), Alan Gilzean (Spurs).

degradations of Scottish football. This, I think, was the worst of all. No wonder the Hampden roar of delight changed to the jeering whistle and the slow handclap.'

Yet, as so often with Scotland, we had the football equivalent of 'the opera isn't over until the fat lady sings'. It was never over with the Scots until the fans were lifted optimistically then sent crashing back to reality. Our last home qualifying game was against Italy in November 1965. Only two minutes of the Hampden game remained when John Greig scored the winner to etch one of the most famous moments in the old stadium's history into football folklore. The Italians were masters of the massed defence and breakaways with stiletto flashes to split open their opponents. Hugh Taylor vividly described the Scotland team's efforts:

'Their hearts pumped and their limbs ached and you could sense the agony as they tried frantically to find superhuman energy. They had played themselves into the ground. They had battered almost non-stop at Italy's majestic defence . . . these were Scotland's World Cup Wonders.'

Sadly, yet again, it all changed. The return match against Italy was in Naples a month later, and half of Scotland's writing corps was on duty. But the Scots team, depleted by injuries to Bill Brown, Billy McNeill, Jim Baxter, Denis Law and Billy Stevenson before the trip, suffered another blow when Rangers winger Willie Henderson controversially called off only half an hour before the kick-off. His Ibrox team-mate Jim

Lost in a sea of blue: John Greig is surrounded by jubilant Scotland team-mates after his winning goal against Italy in the qualifying rounds of the 1966 World Cup.

Neil Martin and Jim Baxter take part in Scotland's victory salute following the win over Italy, 1965.

Forrest took his place and Scotland listed defender Ron Yeats as number 9, but played him in defence. It didn't help. We lost 3–0 and Hugh Taylor wrote sadly: 'Against such a high-class side as Italy only a great slice of luck would have saved Scotland.' Just to rub salt into the wounds England went on to win the World Cup six months later on their own doorstep, and some Scots have never recovered from the shock.

There was no place either for Scotland in the finals line-up in Mexico in 1970, even although the qualifying campaign included an 8–0 victory over Cyprus at Hampden, including four goals for Rangers centre-forward Colin Stein. By this time former Rangers and Queen's Park keeper Bobby Brown was in charge. An ex-St Johnstone manager, Brown took over after John Prentice had briefly succeeded Stein, but became embroiled in a contract dispute with the SFA. Kilmarnock boss Malcolm McDonald had a short two-match spell as caretaker manager before Brown was appointed in February 1967. Despite goals by Jimmy Johnstone and Alan Gilzean the Scots again lost a crunch decider in the qualifying race, this time 3–2 to West Germany in Hamburg, and Tommy Gemmell was sent off.

Brown's prestige never recovered from that defeat and in

Joy at Hampden: team-mates rush to congratulate Willie Henderson after he scores the seventh goal in Scotland's 8–0 defeat of Cyprus in 1969.

Worried looks on the Scotland bench, as they watch a 1–1 draw with Ireland in Dublin in 1969. Lined up left to right are subs Willie Callaghan, Tommy McLean and Bobby Lennox next to manager Bobby Brown and trainer Tom McNiven.

the autumn of 1971 the next manager swept in, the incredible Tommy Docherty. He moved at breathtaking speed to change Scotland's fortunes and, as he had sole control – he didn't have to consult the selection committee – there was never a dull moment.

Docherty led Scotland to a superb 4–1 victory over Denmark in their first match of the qualifying trail for the 1974 finals, which were to be held in West Germany. Goals by Lou Macari, Jimmy Bone, Joe Harper and Willie Morgan got Scotland off to a flying start. They followed this in November

Top managers talk-in, 1967. From left to right: Malcolm Macdonald (Kilmarnock), John Harvey (Hearts), Scot Symon (Rangers), Scotland boss Bobby Brown, Jock Stein (Celtic) and Bob Shankly (Hibs).

1973 with a 2–0 win against the Danes at Hampden, a match which saw the first World Cup goal for Kenny Dalglish. A month later, however, the SFA received an unwanted Christmas present. Docherty quit to become manager of Manchester United with a typical wisecrack: 'As the Mafia say, they made me an offer I couldn't refuse.'

Scotland turned again to St Johnstone, and the Perth club supplied the new international manager, Willie Ormond. His debut was unhappy, the St Valentine's Day massacre at Hampden, with a 5–0 defeat by England in a match which was supposed to celebrate the SFA's centenary.

There was a ten-month gap between the qualifying fixtures before Scotland met old rivals Czechoslovakia at Hampden. And the outcome? Willie Ormond beamed from the front page of the *Record* in the issue of 27 September 1973, lifted on the shoulders of his victorious team, after a wonderful 2–1 victory. Goals by Manchester United defender Jim Holton, an Ormond discovery, and 21-year-old Leeds striker Joe Jordan, finally ended 16 years of the World Cup wilderness for Scotland.

Hugh Taylor claimed that when Jordan scored the winner it unleashed 'the Hampden roar of the century'. And he added: 'Skipper Billy Bremner dashed into the tunnel to bring on manager Willie Ormond for a lap of honour in front of the adoring 100,000 crowd, who had shown no club favour, and bellowed non-stop from start to finish for Scotland.' We were on our way, and so was the Tartan Army. This was the first World Cup in which thousands of Scots fans travelled abroad to support the team, just as their fathers and grandfathers had gone to Wembley.

There were, however, some little local difficulties on the way. Celtic winger Jimmy Johnstone was involved in the famous rowing-boat drama at Largs when he was swept out to sea and had to be rescued. Then Johnstone and Billy Bremner were at the centre of more incidents on a pre-World Cup trip to Norway and Hugh Taylor memorably christened it the '*tour de farce*'. But, true to tradition, the Scots recovered to mount the World Cup campaign of which we can be proudest. The team didn't get to the second stages, but they came so agonisingly close.

The opening game was in Dortmund, a 2–0 victory against the African republic of Zaire. Leeds players Peter

Spying for Scotland: Willie Ormond goes native beside the Sphinx in Egypt on a trip to watch World Cup opponents, Zaire.

Opposite: What's up, Doc? Scotland team boss Tommy Docherty with Asa Hartford before taking off for Copenhagen in 1972.

Lorimer and Joe Jordan scored and, perhaps it was because it was all so new, Taylor wrote: 'We should have won by a bigger margin. There's no doubt about that. But why crib? This was the result we wanted, the result we needed.'

The second game was a superb no-scoring draw against the World Champions Brazil in Frankfurt. Prime Minister Harold Wilson, who flew to watch the game, said, 'I know more about football than politics. Scotland played really well and deserved to win. They should have had a great victory.'

Hugh Taylor marvelled: 'The bagpipes shrilled and the bongo drums were silent as the bravest, brightest Scotland team in years hammered world champions Brazil on to the ropes here tonight.'

Ominously, the back page of 19 June 1974 spelt out the message that Scotland had to beat their next opponents, Yugoslavia, or go out on goal difference. The lack of goals against Zaire was now to prove the trip-wire to the next round for the Scots. But the pre-match message was wrapped in

The Scotland team and officials in a group picture before the 1974 World Cup in West Germany . . . plus skipper Billy Bremner with the team mascot, Rory Superscot.

history. Taylor wrote:

'Tomorrow Scotland face another Bannockburn, with boots on. It will be exactly 660 years to the weekend since Scotland won their greatest victory, a victory that made Scotland a proud and independent nation. If we wish to remain a proud and independent nation on the football pitch, victory is a must against Yugoslavia tomorrow afternoon.'

There were IRA threats to the Scotland team, and gunship helicopters with armed troops trailed the Scots squad's coach and hovered over the stadium.

What players have to do to get their picture in the paper. The tartan line-up is Willie Morgan, Danny McGrain, Billy Bremner, Davie Hay and Sandy Jardine preparing to meet the Czechs.

It was another glorious Scotland failure. We drew 1–1, Jordan scoring two minutes from time, but Brazil, playing Zaire at the same time, pipped Scotland with a vital third goal to take the second qualifying place behind Yugoslavia on goal difference. The section leaders, Brazil and Scotland all finished

Best wishes from the Record *to Scotland's squad in the World Cup in 1974, and thanks from the team.*

Opposite: Ally MacLeod as an Argentinian gaucho before the 1978 finals.

on four points. Taylor summed it up: 'This was a brilliant Scotland team and an unlucky one. One break, and the lads would have been in the finals. Of that I've no doubt.'

Undefeated, but out the World Cup, they flew home to a pop-star welcome in front of 10,000 fans at Glasgow Airport. The *Record*, devoting Page One and the centre pages to the homecoming, reported the words of a German TV commentator who was sent to Glasgow: 'My God. What would it have been like if you had won?'

West Germany was the best of all Scotland's World Cup exploits. It was a talented squad well led off the field by Willie Ormond, and superbly organised on it by Billy Bremner. They really could call themselves unlucky, and two decades on I've never changed that view. But it was followed four years later by the blackest episode of them all: Argentina 1978 still scars the memories of all of us who were involved.

There was a new team manager, the extrovert Ally MacLeod, who guided the Scots to a key 2–0 win against Wales in a match switched to Liverpool's Anfield ground to house a 50,000 crowd. The Tartan Army had reformed in huge numbers for this tie, with nearly all its members on parade. The biggest, blackest type decorated the front page on 13 October 1977: 'YES, WE'RE THERE'. 'The tartan dream has come true,' said the paper. Goals by Don Masson, from a penalty, and Kenny Dalglish, three minutes from time, notched a 2–0 win. There were complaints from the Welsh that the ball had actually been handled by Joe Jordan, not their defender David Jones, so the penalty award was wrong. The incident was replayed countless times on TV in an attempt to show whether French referee Robert Wurtz had made the right or wrong decision. The *Record* was content to leave the last word to Celtic manager Jock Stein, the Godfather of Scottish football: 'I saw the incident six times in the television replay and there was no doubt in my mind that a Welsh player handled,' said Stein. And no one argued with the Big Man!

But the football fates that had a nation rejoicing that night in October had plunged it into unrelieved gloom before the World Cup was finished. It was fun while it lasted, as Ally MacLeod swept the nation along on a cloud of total unreality. The exuberant Ally ignored warning signs that all might not be right with the squad when we could only draw with Northern Ireland and Wales in the British Championship, and lost to

Record-making team: the Scotland squad before they leave for Argentina. Left to right: Willie Donachie, team boss Ally MacLeod, Martin Buchan, Joe Jordan, Sandy Jardine, Bruce Rioch, Derek Johnstone, Asa Hartford and John Blackley.

England. Nor did he consider it necessary to look at any of our group opponents in Argentina.

On the evening of their departure to South America the squad paraded at a huge send-off party at Hampden, for which the fans had to pay to get into the ground – the first time a lap of honour has been held *before* an event. They didn't dare hold one on their return: they would have been stoned to death. Although the flak flew at MacLeod for such a ludicrous idea, the scheme wasn't his – it had come from inside the SFA.

Grim reality struck on the night of Saturday, 3 June 1978. Scotland lost 3–1 to Peru in Cordoba, although Jordan had put the Scots ahead, then Masson missed a penalty. The stories were wrapped in black borders by Monday. Alex Cameron wrote:

'Scotland lost 3–1 to the so-called Dad's Army from Peru in an incredible shambles which yesterday turned their training camp into a morgue, and had fingers pointing at manager Ally MacLeod. Lack of briefing and the wrong tactical approach were the recurring whispers as players scurried to get away from the public misery.'

And in a Sports Opinion viewpoint, Cameron argued: 'Ally's Army is on the march and looking for blood. The irate reaction from fans who feel badly let down is fully understandable. But what we need now is restraint and dignity. Surely the time for assessing blame is after the

matches against Iran and Holland.'

But the writer might as well have stood underneath the Niagara Falls hoping an umbrella would keep him dry. Between the time of that article being written and the paper hitting the streets the next morning a new sensation had blasted its way on to Page One: 'World Cup star Willie Johnston plunged Scotland into a drugs scare last night. A test made on him immediately after the defeat by Peru proved positive.' Johnston, off the field one of the quietest players in the squad, was sent home in disgrace for taking medication with a banned substance in it. Maybe he was fortunate – he got out of Argentina early.

After the second result, a 1–1 draw with unrated Iran – and only an own-goal by the opposition giving Scotland that draw – soccer hell broke loose. The story filled the front, middle and back pages. 'FANS STONE TEAM BUS', reported the *Record* and a Page One opinion reflected the fury of the nation: 'Cry for us Argentina. For last night was the bitter end.' Rows between the SFA and the players over bonuses then emerged, and as Scotland supporters in Argentina vented their wrath it was only matched by the anger back home.

The next day in the team training camp, a hotel in Alta Gracia which had seen better days, manager MacLeod admitted: 'I know I will not survive this. The knives are out for me. I take the blame, but I'm still amazed and unbelieving that so many players could lose their form at the same time. I simply hope we can put it all together against Holland, but it is a pretty dismal prospect.'

The lap of honour before the dishonour: the Scotland players parade at Hampden the night they left for Argentina, 1978.

Jet pace from superstar Diego Maradona as he sweeps past Scotland defender Paul Hegarty, 1979.

It wouldn't be Scotland if there wasn't a twist to the plot. Graeme Souness, left out for the two previous games, was brought into the team and he helped inspire MacLeod's dejected troops. Page One was cleared again for the story of the game against Holland. A subheading said: 'We're out! But boy was it close.' That lead to the banner headline: 'THANKS FOR A FIGHTING FINISH'. The *Record* reported:

'Scotland, as expected, went out the World Cup last night. But, at last, we gained some pride. Our team beat the fancied Dutch 3–2 and in typically infuriating fashion we go out on goal difference, thanks to the disasters against Peru and Iran.

'But the performance against Holland was magnificent. And the same fans who jeered the team four days ago cheered them to the echo last night.'

Amazingly Scotland had come so close to qualifying for the second round. Kenny Dalglish scored and Archie Gemmill

got two, one from a penalty, and one voted the goal of the tournament. That second Gemmill goal put the Scots 3–1 ahead, but Johnny Rep scored Holland's vital second to edge through on goal difference and, as Alex Cameron lamented, 'Sadly, it all came too late.'

Ally MacLeod survived a vote of confidence after the World Cup finals, but it only delayed the inevitable. The manager, who had been the pied piper of the nation, eventually quit in the autumn of 1978 to return to the first club he had been in charge of, Ayr United.

So the SFA turned yet again to Jock Stein. He had moved to Leeds United after an unhappy episode when he quit as Celtic manager only for the Parkhead club to snub him in incredible fashion by offering him the post of lottery manager. 'Gentlemen, meet our new manager from England,' said SFA secretary Ernie Walker at the press conference introducing Stein. There was a marked contrast in styles. Flamboyance was

Tactics talk: Scotland skipper Archie Gemmill, manager Jock Stein and Graeme Souness discuss plans.

Three of the best: Liverpool Scots Kenny Dalglish, Alan Hansen and Graeme Souness at an international training session.

out, common sense was in. The backstage rows that had marred Argentina were ended. One of the biggest had been about bonus payments. These were now settled before the qualifying games began.

The aim was to qualify for Spain in 1982, in a World Cup extended from 16 to 24 finalists. Scotland found themselves in a five-nation group, along with Northern Ireland, Sweden, Portugal and Israel. We got off to a flyer, with a 1–0 win when Gordon Strachan scored against Sweden in Stockholm. Scotland never looked back, and went on to finish top of the section.

The paper, as ever, catered for its readers – thousands of whom had joined the Tartan Army for the latest expedition to Spain. A back-page logo proclaimed 'World Cup *Record*' and carried an announcement under it: 'On sale today in Spain. Price 100 pesetas.' The *Record* had arranged an air-lift so readers wouldn't be deprived of their favourite paper, on sale in Spain the day of publication.

Scotland's first game was against no-hopers New Zealand in Malaga. But playing also-rans had proved dangerous for the Scots in the past, and it would be so again. The story of the game was recorded on the back page under the headline 'ANGRY STEIN'. It went on: 'Scotland won their World Cup opener 5–2 over New Zealand. It was only the third victory by a Scottish side in the final stages, following on the '74 success over Zaire and the '78 triumph over Holland.'

But it was so nearly a re-run of the game against Zaire eight years earlier. A Dalglish goal and a double by John Wark gave us a 3–0 lead, then Scotland nearly pulled defeat from the jaws of victory by letting the Kiwis storm back to 3–2. Late goals by John Robertson and Steve Archibald may have given the score-line a better gloss, but this time everyone knew the significance of the two goals conceded, including the manager. Stein blasted: 'We lost goals because of self-inflicted wounds. We are the greatest nation in the world for punishing ourselves at every turn.'

It was on to the searing heat of Seville for the second match, and another World Cup meeting with Brazil. But there was no repeat of the '74 draw as Scotland were beaten 4–1. Alex Cameron commented: 'It was no disgrace for Scotland to lose as they did. Few teams in the world, if indeed any at all, would have lived in such a cauldron of heat with a team of such driving finishers.' The Scots' solitary goal was a memorable first international strike for David Narey which went into football history when TV pundit Jimmy Hill – always the Scots' number-one enemy – called it a 'toe-poke', a distinctly odd description of a goal which Cameron described as a shot swirling into the top right-hand corner.

Scotland had to beat Russia in the final game, but again the hoodoo of goal difference wrecked their dreams. Alex Cameron reported sorrowfully from Malaga:

'Scotland are out of the World Cup with the hard-luck story to beat them all. The end could not have been more dramatic if it had been scripted.

'Out near the touchline Alan Hansen and Willie Miller went desperately for the ball. As Miller shaped to

We're off to sunny Spain. The Scotland squad get ready to board the plane to take them to the 1982 World Cup Finals.

clear, Hansen collided with him and the ball broke to Russia's striker and player of the year, Ramaz Shengelia. Alan Rough saw what was happening and began to run out of his goal. Then he hesitated and began to move back. Shengelia did a broad sweep away from the keeper and then shot into an empty goal.'

That was in the 85th minute. No matter that a minute later Graeme Souness equalised for a final score of 2–2, Jordan having given the Scots a half-time lead, Jock Stein's men were out of the World Cup. Cameron summed it up: 'It is not another Argentina story. The Scots players will fly home tomorrow and they have no reason to be ashamed of their performances.'

Jock Stein was realistic: 'I don't think it's ever really imaginable that we could win the World Cup. It would be almost impossible for a country of our size. It's a dream, but we always hope to do well.' The Spanish campaign had not been like Argentina. News reporters sent to focus on players' revels found themselves with plenty of time to sunbathe. There was no trouble from the fans, either. They had a ball, but not one arrest was made. There were no front-page stories – just as well for harassed night editors as there was another conflict going on at the same time. It was called the Falklands War.

Jock Stein was retained for a second World Cup qualifying round, and this time the 1986 finals would return to Mexico. Scotland proved again it is better to travel hopefully than to arrive. Their peak performances were reserved for the qualifying campaigns, and few have been better than the 3–1 Hampden demolition of Spain with a double strike by a new World Cup hit-man, Celtic's Mo Johnston, and another goal by the old master, Kenny Dalglish.

But it was a rocky road to Mexico, and in the end it meant another show-down with Wales who decided this time to play on their own territory, Ninian Park, Cardiff. A win would take Scotland through, a draw give them a two-game play-off with Australia. They got that draw with a 1–1 result, but for once the game was totally eclipsed by another event. The *Record*'s Page One of 11 September 1985 carried the headline 'JOCK STEIN DEAD', and I reported:

'Jock Stein, the Big Man of Scottish football, died last night – in the very moment of his latest triumph. The 62-year-old Scotland manager had a heart attack as his team

Congratulations from Mo Johnston (left) to Charlie Nicholas after the Arsenal striker scored the last goal in Scotland's 6–1 defeat of Yugoslavia in 1984.

clawed their way back from World Cup disaster.'

The main leader, written by sports editor Charles Smith, summed it up:

'Jock Stein died as he lived – a winner. The Lanarkshire miner, who became the greatest manager in Scottish football, seemed indestructible. Last night would have been one of his greatest moments. But, tragically, a black-edged year for football claimed its most famous victim. The Big Man of Scottish football leaves a gap that can never be filled.'

Before he collapsed, the manager had seen substitute Davie Cooper equalise with a penalty for Scotland nine minutes from time. That tied the score at 1–1, Mark Hughes having scored a 13th-minute goal for Wales. Cooper took the kick as Wales bitterly protested about the award. For the second time in a crunch World Cup tie with Scotland they thought they had been robbed. Alex Cameron wrote the epitaph on the game: 'For sheer grit and determination this was one of Scotland's nights to remember. What a tragedy that Stein was not spared to savour it.'

Aberdeen manager Alex Ferguson, who had been Stein's part-time number two, was appointed to look after the international side, while still retaining his role at Pittodrie. His squad survived the long trip to Australia, and returned with a goalless draw which meant that Frank McAvennie's goal in the 1–0 win at Hampden sent Scotland into their fourth successive World Cup finals.

Scotland, with Ferguson as manager, were in Group E in the World Cup, nicknamed the 'Group of Death' as it included defeated finalists from the previous tournament, West Germany, plus rising European power Denmark, and temperamental South Americans Uruguay.

The Scots made a dismal start, being beaten 1–0 by Denmark, and Alex Cameron reported from Mexico City:

'Scotland will need a soccer miracle to survive the World Cup's "Group of Death" after tumbling to a single-goal defeat at the Neza Stadium in the heart of the city's slumland. The task now facing the Scots against West Germany and Uruguay seems hopelessly out of their reach.'

But it didn't look that way for four marvellous minutes in the heat of Queretaro on a Sunday afternoon, when Gordon

Strachan put Scotland ahead in 17 minutes. But Rudi Völler equalised four minutes later and Klaus Allofs gave the Germans another shortly after the interval. I reported:

'Scotland's players sweated pounds as they plunged to their second World Cup defeat. Team boss Alex Ferguson revealed: "All my players have lost weight, some of them as much as 8 lbs during the match. I reckon skipper Graeme Souness has been the worst affected."'

There was a grim warning for Scotland when I travelled to the West German squad's training camp and one of their stars, Pierre Littbarski, spoke about Gordon Strachan, who had emerged as Scotland's star. Under the headline 'MY FEARS FOR STRACHAN', he said of the Uruguayans: 'They will simply chop him down if he beats them. I just pray he is not seriously injured.'

Off to the World Cup, 1986. The men in charge of the Scotland squad for the Finals in Mexico. Front row: Manager Alex Ferguson, assistant Walter Smith. Second row: Archie Knox, Teddy Scott, Craig Brown. Third row: Jim Steel, Dr Stewart Hillis, Hugh Allan, Andy Roxburgh. Back: Eric Ferguson.

Littbarski proved correct about the Uruguyan tackling, but even he couldn't have imagined how little time it took them to act. Only 40 seconds had ticked away before Jose Batista chopped down Strachan and was sent off by French referee Joel Quiniou. Alex Cameron hit out: 'Uruguay's tactics bring disrepute to their title of South American champions.'

But Scotland could not take advantage of playing against ten men and the match finished in a no-scoring draw. The incident also sparked off the most amazing outburst by SFA secretary Ernie Walker, with words which, if any club manager had said them, would have led to the SFA disciplining him immediately. Under a back-page headline 'BUTCHERED BY

CHEATS!' Walker told me: 'That was no game of football out there today. There were ten cheats and cowards, the scum of world football.'

Team boss Ferguson weighed in, branding the South Americans 'a disgrace to world football'. But in an after-match press conference which turned into a shambles, Uruguyan manager Omar Borras said of Batista's sending-off: 'The referee was a murderer.'

Ferguson had made a controversial team selection, leaving out skipper Graeme Souness who had recently been appointed player-manager at Rangers and putting 21-year-old Paul McStay in his place. The war of words between the manager and his skipper rumbled on and Ferguson admitted to the *Record*: 'I know he feels badly about not playing and it wasn't an easy decision to drop the captain. But three games in nine days was a very punishing schedule for anyone in mid-field.'

Souness said to me: 'He's the manager and I have to accept his decision although it choked me. I think Alex was wrong. It was a game for experience. I could have played, and I wanted to play. I've no intention of changing my mind. I won't be playing for Scotland again.' And he never did.

Alex Cameron summed up a World Cup where Scotland had never really looked like making an impact:

'It would be churlish not to concede that had Scotland to meet Argentina we might have been slaughtered. Major failure is up front. Games can't be won consistently with forwards who score every blue moon.

'Canada were the only country who didn't score in the 36 opening games and our tally of one – by Strachan against West Germany – was matched by those great soccer powers Algeria and Iraq. The supporters who travelled, and behaved well, deserved better.'

Scotland changed managers yet again for the 1990 finals in Italy. The SFA turned their back on club managers and controversially promoted their coaching boss, Andy Roxburgh, to be the international chief. The Scots were in a five-nation group along with Yugoslavia, France, Norway and Cyprus, and they made a good start with a 2–1 victory against the Norwegians in Oslo, thanks to goals by Paul McStay and Mo Johnston. One of the highlights of the qualifying campaign was a winner by Richard Gough against minnows Cyprus in

Limassol to grab a 3–2 victory, six minutes into injury-time. The normally undemonstrative Roxburgh danced a jig of joy on the touchline. And in the next match the Scots powered to a 2–0 win against the star-studded French, Johnston scoring both goals.

But the hopes raised by finishing runners-up to leaders Yugoslavia in the qualifying group were swept away in the first game in the finals. It was a disaster worse than Peru in 1978 and under the back-page headline 'DOWN AND OUTS', I reported on 12 June 1990 from Genoa:

'Andy Roxburgh gave his grim verdict last night after Scotland had been humbled 1–0 by unrated Costa Rica in our worst World Cup disaster. "We hold up our hands. We've no excuses," said the ashen-faced manager. "The players are shattered, we're all bitterly disappointed."'

Alex Cameron pulled no punches:

'Scotland were humiliated with the whole wide world watching yesterday. They were beaten by a team of nobodies who were so surprised at the finish that their joy matched winning the World Cup itself. It is the worst defeat Scotland have ever suffered in the World Cup finals. They were a disgrace.'

Record readers in the Sports Hotline column agreed, phoning in the views on the disaster result. One said: 'Costa Rica are supposed to be a third world football nation. If that's the case Scotland couldn't beat an egg.' And another summed it up: 'That was a shambles and a disgrace. I'm away to have a good drink.'

The nightmare of Argentina, with its off-the-field dramas, looked as if it might be set for a revival. Firstly Rangers defender Richard Gough, who had played for only 45 minutes against Costa Rica, had to fly home with a foot injury. Much worse was to follow, as the *Record* reported on Thursday, 14 June 1990: 'Scotland coach Andy Roxburgh yesterday vehemently denied two of his World Cup stars were drunk on a night out.'

Mo Johnston and Jim Bett were the players accused, but Roxburgh insisted no disciplinary action would be taken. 'Why should there be? There is no breach of rules here.'

And true to form, after a week of dismal stories and headlines, Scotland bounced back with a 2–1 victory over Sweden in Genoa and Alex Cameron enthused:

Opposite: Scotland debut for Gary McAllister, in the 1990 game against East Germany.

'As one of Scotland's most partisan critics I was over-whelmed with delight. If Scotland had attacked Costa Rica in the same fashion they would have swept them into the Mediterranean within minutes.

'Stuart McCall – the new Billy Bremner – has established himself as a star international after only seven appearances for Scotland. The Leeds-born 26-year-old teamed up with penalty ace Mo Johnston to score in the super 2–1 World Cup victory over Sweden and bring Scotland galloping back into the running in our Group C crunch with Brazil at Turin on Wednesday.'

But that match ended in a 1–0 victory for the South Americans and on Page One the *Record* reported:

'The Tartan Army were left in tears again last night – by the one that got away. Scotland's football heroes needed just a single point to qualify for the knock-out stages of the World Cup for the very first time. But soccer wizards Brazil scored seven minutes from the end to virtually destroy our chances.'

Cameron reported:

'Scotland were desperately unlucky to lose to the might of Brazil at the Alpi Stadium last night. If only Taffarel hadn't made that super save from Johnston. The striker was on the six-yard line when Stuart McCall headed a centre from McKimmie back across goal. Johnston met it well, but the acrobatic keeper jumped to divert the shot over.'

So it was goodbye to Italia '90. Andy Roxburgh was kept as team boss, or 'coach', as the SFA termed him, for the next qualifying campaign, and the target was USA '94.

Before that, Roxburgh enjoyed the real high noon of his spell as Scotland boss, in the 1992 European Championships in Sweden. The Scots had never before qualified for the finals, and the predictions were gloomy. They lost 1–0 to reigning European Champions, Holland, and 2–0 to reigning World Champions, Germany, then finished with a 3–0 victory over CIS a – with goals from the merry Macs, Paul McStay, Brian McClair and Gary McAllister. Skipper Richard Gough told the *Record* after that third game win: 'We did it for our wonderful fans. They deserved a result like this for the backing they've given us.'

And in a post-Euro summing-up I wrote:

'The front-page headline in one of Sweden's leading papers said it all. Printed in English it read "THANK YOU, SCOTLAND". Andy Roxburgh's squad of so-called no-hopers, written off by English-based papers, returned with the best record since Willie Ormond's men just failed to reach the last stages of the 1974 World Cup. I was there that year – and I've been with Scotland in every major competition since. This lot are up with the best.

'Scotland kicked into touch the "boring" tag which had followed them for 12 months. Fans stayed away in droves from the warm-up games – but if we were playing at Hampden next week the queues would start today.'

Alex Cameron praised the team manager and said, 'Roxburgh and his number two, Craig Brown, deserve at least as much credit as the marvellous Richard Gough and his team.'

Hopes were high this would mark a real turning-point for the international side. Gordon Strachan said we must have

Getting on target: Gordon Durie, watched by Brian McClair and Gary McAllister, in a training session in Sweden for the European Championships.

Andy Roxburgh's stress level soars during a Scotland international at Pittodrie.

*You're the man! That seems
to be the message from
Andy Roxburgh to Rangers
striker Ally McCoist who –
as ever – sees the funny side
of it all.*

Scotland skipper Gary McAllister (left) with team-mates Pat Nevin and Colin Hendry before the World Cup qualifying game in Malta in 1993.

Previous page: Salute to the fans from Andy Roxburgh at the end of the World Cup victory against Sweden in 1990.

every chance of making it to the 1994 finals in America. But Scotland's attempts never got off the launching-pad, starting with a defeat by Switzerland in Berne in which skipper Richard Gough was sent off. By the end of it Scotland's hopes were gone, Gough was gone – saying he refused ever to play under Roxburgh again – and so was Roxburgh.

New manager Craig Brown stepped up from the number-two role. His aim is to qualify for France in 1998, for the days when legislators, and writers, could regard the World Cup with disdain belong to football's prehistoric age. Hopefully there will be no repeat of those World Cup lean years between 1958 and 1974 while we watched from the outside. But that will be another chapter!

Five Scotland stars of the future. From left to right: Christian Dailly, David Hannah, Steven Pressley, Simon Donnelly and Stewart Kerr.

Next page: Crunch! As Brian McClair tries to force his way through against Northern Ireland in a friendly international at Hampden.

Raging Bulls

Boxing Heroes

One hundred years from now a book on the next century of Scottish sport may have only a slim chapter on boxing. It is the sport which is under most attack, and has an uncertain future. But more than most sports it also dwells lovingly in the past, and what a past it has been. Men who battled their way out of the slums to fight for their next meal. The eternal Scottish sporting hero, who soared to the top with the swagger that ignited the crowds, and then tumbled to the bottom, destroying himself in the process.

No one typified this more than the greatest of them all, Benny Lynch. It's 60 years since the little man with magic in his feet and dynamite in his fists won the world flyweight championship, only to die 11 years later a down-and-out alcoholic. It had the stamp of a Hollywood script for a 1930s' movie, with James Cagney in the starring role.

Yet six decades later the ghost of Lynch lives on. Old men remember, and it has spawned a play about his turbulent life and books tracing the rise and fall of the champ from the Gorbals who is still hailed as one of the greatest sporting stars Scotland produced this century.

There always remains the fatal fascination of the lifestyle that destroyed him. As one observer of the fight scene wrote, 'He excited a depressed Glasgow by turning the minds of the

Opposite: World Champ, with all the style: Benny Lynch and his wife, Anne, strolling through Glasgow.

Settled with a handshake: Benny Lynch and his new manager, George Dingley, agree to a contract.

unemployed from the grim facts of life and showing them with wonderful panache what one of their own kind could do. When they watched him they escaped with him from their miserable surroundings.'

It was on 9 September 1935 that Lynch blasted his way into Scotland's sporting history. He won the World, European and British flyweight championships when he beat the holder, Jackie Brown of Manchester, in that city's Belle Vue arena. And

Lynch didn't just take the titles, he grabbed them from Brown in an incredible 4 minutes and 42 seconds of the scheduled 15 rounds. And before the end came 1 minute and 42 seconds into that second round, Lynch had floored Brown an incredible eight times.

That second-round victory catapulted him on to the front page of the *Daily Record*. 'Scotland's first World Champion. Lynch wins inside two rounds,' it proclaimed. The triumphant report was by Elky Clark who, the paper reminded its readers, had fought for the title which Lynch had won.

Curiously, Lynch's success wasn't the lead story. That belonged to an account of the shooting of the controversial American politician, Senator Huey Long – an important event, but hardly the big talking point that morning in the Gorbals where Lynch came from. However, for the cost of one penny, the paper tried to make it up to its readers elsewhere. The back page was almost completely given over to Lynch, and there was a picture of his young wife. Inside, Elky Clark, billed as the ex-European flyweight champion, detailed the story of the fight, and, with it ending so quickly, it almost was a blow-by-blow account: 'The champion seemed helpless under the terrific onslaught. Lynch threw Brown out of his stride and then began to ply that deadly left hook of his at every opportunity.'

'It seems all too wonderful,' said Lynch in his dressing-room after the fight. And readers were told how he had gained experience in the boxing-booths of the time: 'Many times he fought twice in the same night against men heavier than himself.' He came home to a hero's reception, and Glasgow and Scotland belonged to Lynch.

Though it was a time of great harshness in society, it was gentler towards the character flaws of the famous which were rarely paraded by the press. Just as well for Lynch, who would surely have made Page One for the wrong reasons. Boxing expert John Blair, later to be the paper's writer on the sport, is a tremendous admirer of the wee man. 'I've never seen a boxer as good as him,' he recalls. 'But just after the world title win I remember seeing a man standing at the corner of Rutherglen Road and Crown Street in the Gorbals with an expensive white silk scarf round his neck. He was waving a wine bottle above his head and shouting he would fight anyone who wanted to take him on. I was only a teenager and it made a tremendous impression on me. It was Benny Lynch.'

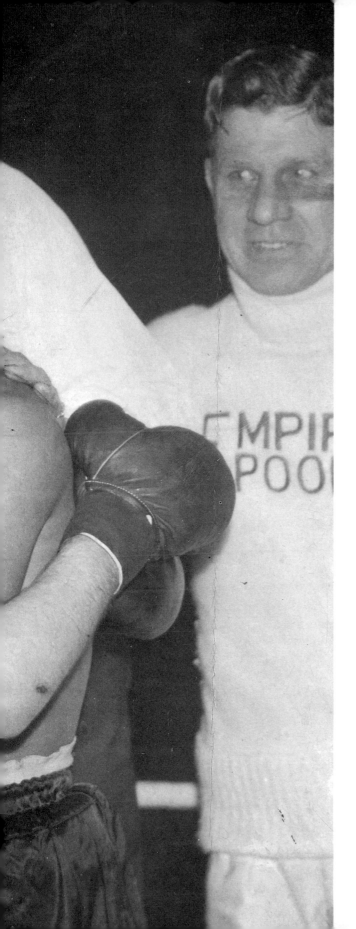

*Great fight! Benny Lynch
and Small Montana
embrace at the end of the
Scot's victory at the Empire
Pool, Wembley.*

The champion made a successful defence of his title at Shawfield on 16 September 1936, when he knocked out Londoner Pat Palmer in eight rounds in front of 35,000 'wildly excited fans who saw Lynch account for his game challenger with two of the best left-hook deliveries I have seen,' said Elky Clark.

Again he didn't make the main story on Page One. A political crisis in Portugal, of all places, beat him to it. But for his next world title defence the paper pulled out all the stops. His points victory over the American, Small Montana, at the Empire Pool, Wembley, on 19 January 1937 was splashed all over the front page. Lynch received £2,600 for his night's work and he was hailed by Elky Clark as the 'undisputed flyweight champion of the world'. 'Benny has always been noted as a fighter depending mostly on a big punch to bring him victory but on this display tonight he surprised his most ardent admirers by the way he boxed and brought into play a clever craftsmanship.'

The actress Billie Houston, one of the Houston sisters famous at the time, was drafted on to Page One and started: 'Well, Gorbals have it.' And she went on, presumably to a mercifully unnamed ghost-writer: 'I wanted Gorbals to win, and it did win. How I wanted Lynch to win. And he won. So here's to us.'

Waverley wrote he had a telephone conversation with Benny in the early hours of the morning, and he was determined not to miss anything out.

'"How are you, Benny?" I queried.

"I'm feeling very fit. Let me give this message to the *Daily Record*. I'm not the least bit damaged and I'm mighty proud that once again I have won for Scotland. Just now I feel proud I am a Scot, and that I have kept the title for my country."

'Tommy Morgan, the famous Scots comedian, who is a close friend of Benny, was with me during the conversation. He also had a word with the champion. "We're all waiting to give you a great welcome," said Tommy.'

The *Record* went one better for Lynch's next fight against Peter Kane, signing up British heavyweight star Tommy Farr who had just returned from America after a brave attempt to take the world title from the fabulous Joe Louis. He would report the title defence. That *was* Page One news, and the readers were assured he has 'a ready wit and a pleasing style. His unrivalled knowledge of the finer points of the game will make his report of supreme value to all followers of the "noble art".'

And the next morning, 14 October 1937, after Lynch had knocked Kane out in the 13th round in front of 30,000 fans at Shawfield, Farr said on Page One: 'It was a hectic battle, every round, and the best fight, honestly, I have ever seen. Lynch reserved his strength the better and it did the trick. He was a worthy champion and punched too correctly and too hard for his gallant opponent.'

And a news report on the back page described the fight as 'one of the greatest ring battles ever fought in Scotland. The fight will go into ring history as an epic. The scenes which accompanied Lynch's magnificent victory will be unforgettable.'

Film star Victor McLaglen was at the ringside accompanying Tommy Farr and both men were deluged by autograph-hunters. When Lynch won, the reporter said: 'Outside the ropes, hats, programmes, anything the fans could lay their hands on, were tossed in the air.' One fan collapsed and died from a heart-attack, another crashed through the roof of the covered enclosure, falling 20 feet and landing on spectators below, one of them being knocked unconscious.

Lynch was carried shoulder-high from the ring, but it was the last hurrah for him at world-title level. His next fight was not until 29 June 1938, against the American Jackie Jurich of California, at Love Street, Paisley. Elky Clark started his fight preview with a distinct lack of confidence:

'In boxing you must be prepared for freak results but I think we'll find Benny Lynch still world flyweight champion this time tomorrow morning.

'Lynch has had a big fight during his training. Probably Old Man Weight has given him as big a fight as he'll get from his opponent of tonight. But I haven't the least doubt Lynch will weigh-in today with O.M.W. flat on his back for the full count, and no ounces that shouldn't be there.'

Clark was a seasoned observer who knew his boxing, and perhaps it was loyalty to Lynch that had misled him. The old *Daily Record* office in Hope Street, where spectators could stand outside the building and watch the papers being printed, was at the centre of one of the saddest episodes in Scotland's sporting history. It was called Newspaper House before the war, renamed Kemsley House and then Record House after the war. And on a June afternoon in 1938 the Glasgow landmark was the venue where Benny Lynch lost his world title. Not in the ring, with at least the consolation he had fought and lost, but at the weigh-in which was held in the *Record* offices. Waverley graphically described the scene:

'As soon as I looked at Lynch I knew he was overweight. If I hadn't seen him I could still have told by the haggard expression on the face of Puggy Morgan, his trainer.

'He was called to the scales by Mr Charles Donmall, secretary of the British Boxing Board of Control, about two o'clock in the afternoon. Lynch stood on the scales with his hands clasped behind his back, a defiant sort of expression on his face. Secretary Donmall moved the measure up and down. "Step off," he said. Lynch moved off the scales and immediately there was a round of applause. Those in the hall thought he was "under". Donmall raised his hand for silence. Then, unemotionally, he announced Benny's weight, 6½ pounds over the stipulated 8 stone. There was a gasp of amazement.

'"He hasn't even made bantamweight," I heard someone mutter. I watched promoter George Dingley. He was stunned. He looked as if he had taken a left hook on the solar from Lynch.

'Crowds milled outside the office. And inside the dethroned champion's wife on the verge of collapse. The worry of it all. Benny, meanwhile, was in a restaurant having his first solid meal in days. And he was in tears.'

A non-title fight eventually went ahead and the saddest introduction on a Benny Lynch fight report began:

'Ex-world champion Benny Lynch knocked out Californian Jackie Jurich in the twelfth round of their contest at Love Street, Paisley, last night, which was to have been for the Scot's world flyweight title – but Jurich took the honours. The American's grand display made it all the more regrettable that the fight was robbed of its title status by Lynch's lapse at the weigh-in.'

There were no more Page One mentions for Lynch until the morning of Wednesday, 7 August 1946, when the paper reported:

'Benny Lynch died suddenly in the Southern General Hospital, Glasgow, last night. He was taken to the hospital shortly after five o'clock and three hours later succumbed to his illness. He was 33 years of age and is survived by his wife and two children. Just over a week ago Benny Lynch fought in a boxing booth in Glasgow Green.'

It was a time of strict post-war newsprint rationing, and the *Record* was reduced to a mere eight pages. Yet it looks strange today that the paper's report on the funeral was only a tiny four paragraphs, under the headline: '2,000 PAY LAST TRIBUTE TO BENNY LYNCH'. But then again, perhaps there was nothing more to be said about a man who had reached sport's heavenly heights, and ended in the depths. He could tame any flyweight in the world, except himself.

The next Scot to step onto the world stage was another little big man, Jackie Paterson. He held the world flyweight title for even longer than Lynch, from 19 June 1943 until 23 March 1948.

Paterson won the title at Hampden against Lynch's old opponent, Peter Kane, with one of the most spectacular knock-outs in world championship history, only 61 seconds after the bell to start the fight had sounded.

It was billed as a world title fight. But, of course, another global contest was going at the same time, the Second World War. And with nearly all of Europe under Nazi rule and much of the Far East dominated by Japan, it now looks a pretty empty title. The real battles were fought with guns, not boxing-gloves.

Space was so tight in war-restricted newspapers that the *Record* could only devote four paragraphs, in its smallest print, to the victory of Paterson, who was a corporal in the RAF. Elky Clark considered Paterson to be too good for any of his likely rivals and lamented, 'It would be a promoter's dream if he could find an opponent that would test the world champion.'

It was after the war before Paterson defended his title, against Liverpool's Joe Curran at Hampden Park. A crowd of 45,000 for the fight on 10 July 1946 paid prices ranging from five shillings (25p) to £3.3s (£3.15).

But the weight problems that were to haunt Paterson's reign had begun to show themselves. In his preview Clark

Ready for action: Jackie Paterson shows the power which made him a champion.

Jackie Paterson (a sergeant in the RAF), with one of the most famous Scots of them all, Sir Harry Lauder, at a war-time meeting with an admirer.

warned: 'For the first time in many years the title-holder is not a safe bet. His "boiling down" to make the flyweight poundage of 8 stone is bound to sap some of his strength.'

However, the *Record* reported triumphantly the next morning. 'Joe Curran's boast that he would finish off Jackie Paterson was a baseless thing. Paterson retained his World, Empire and British flyweight titles in a manner that made his challenger look second class.'

The champion won on points, but there was a gap of nearly two years before his next defence, against Rinty Monaghan of Northern Ireland in that famous arena, the King's Hall, Belfast. By this time Paterson's weight was topic number one. A week before the fight he weighed 8 stone, 4 pounds and 8 ounces, and Elky Clark warned:

'I doubt if he will be strong enough to beat the Irish crooner-boxer. Jackie, however, is confident he'll make the weight and just as sure that he'll be strong, but I doubt that. Only once in my career was I over the 8 stone 2 pound mark four days before a title fight. That was against Fidel La Barba for the world championship and my weight reducing meant that I could not drink water for three weeks before the fight.'

Paterson did make the weight, but in order to do so, as Peter Wilson recalled:

'He spent the previous night literally sweating off the pounds in front of a furnace in Glasgow before he arrived in Belfast. He was so weak he had almost to be carried onto the scales for the weigh-in. Paterson was counted out against Rinty Monaghan, one leg folded up under him like a sheet of paper, physically conscious but so weak as to be utterly incapable of rising.'

'I've finished with flyweight contests,' said Paterson, and his next world-title fight was on 26 October 1949 when, again at Hampden, he fought the Mexican Manuel Ortiz for the bantamweight crown. Again Peter Wilson looked back:

'The fight was not so memorable for Paterson was outpointed rather too easily, but the circumstances were. The fight was held at Hampden and great barricades of snow were banked by the side of the pitch. I cannot remember ever feeling colder in my life and what Ortiz, who had done most of his fighting in sunny California, must have felt I cannot imagine.

'But he had one unique defence that night. He was smothered in blankets between rounds. When he came out to fight his body heat and his breath literally produced a "steam screen" which had Paterson punching as vagrantly as though he had been blind-folded.'

That was almost the end of Paterson's newsworthiness, until November 1966 when a grim Page One story began:

'Jackie Paterson, one of Scotland's boxing greats, has been murdered in South Africa. The 47-year-old former world flyweight champion bled to death after being stabbed with a broken bottle. Paterson's death is a shock for Scots fight fans, felt all the more because it comes just a week after the death of Chic Calderwood in a road accident.'

His 74-year-old father Rab, who lived in Dennistoun, Glasgow, said: 'I always had the feeling that something terrible would happen to Jackie, that he would die before me. He was a great fighter – but oh, what a fool with money.'

Paterson was reckoned to have earned £83,000 in his boxing career and Hugh Taylor (who had helped Paterson write his autobiography) in his obituary on the former butcher's boy from Springside, Ayrshire, said:

'He was the quietest, most unassuming of men. You could

hardly believe he was concerned with weight problems, gambling debts and bankruptcy. He caught the gambling bug more badly than any athlete I've known.

'Jackie received his money in the afternoon. At night he put the lot on at a dog track, and trebled the sum. "Don't worry," Jackie told me. "I'm using the money to buy a business." Little did I know he was going into the bookmaking business. That was like a compulsive drinker buying a pub, and soon Jackie was bankrupt.

'Now he's dead. But I'll always remember him as a magnificent champion and a fine sportsman.'

Earlier that year, on 14 June 1966, Walter McGowan, the third Scot to win the world flyweight title, captured his crown. I was proud to be at the ringside at the Empire Pool, Wembley, to see him join the all-time Scottish greats. In a fascinating feature on the day of the fight Dick Currie, a former Empire Games gold medallist and by then the *Record*'s respected boxing writer, traced the link between Scotland and the world flyweight title.

'As McGowan, from Burnbank, Lanarkshire, battles to take the title away from Salvatore Burruni, it will become more than just another world-title fight to thousands of Scottish boxing fans. To them, Walter's battle to reach the top has been a boxing crusade with only one aim: to win the one world title Scotland feels is her own. In the white heat of this furnace of fight talent iron men were made, men whose names ring out like the proud battle honours of our finest regiments: Johnny Hill, Elky Clark, Benny Lynch, Jackie Paterson.

'McGowan's father and manager, Joe Gans, will hope that lady luck smiles more kindly on his boy than she did on Johnny Hill and Elky Clark. Hill was the uncrowned king of the world's flyweights yet never won the crown because the Americans recognised their own champion, Frankie Genaro. Brave little Elky Clark, later to become the *Daily Record*'s boxing writer, got his title chance when he was 29. Elky, British and European flyweight champion and Scottish bantamweight champion, went to New York to fight Italian-American Fidel La Barba in Madison Square Garden on 21 January 1927. The fight for the vacant world title was over the strange distance of 12 rounds, and the little Glasgow battler

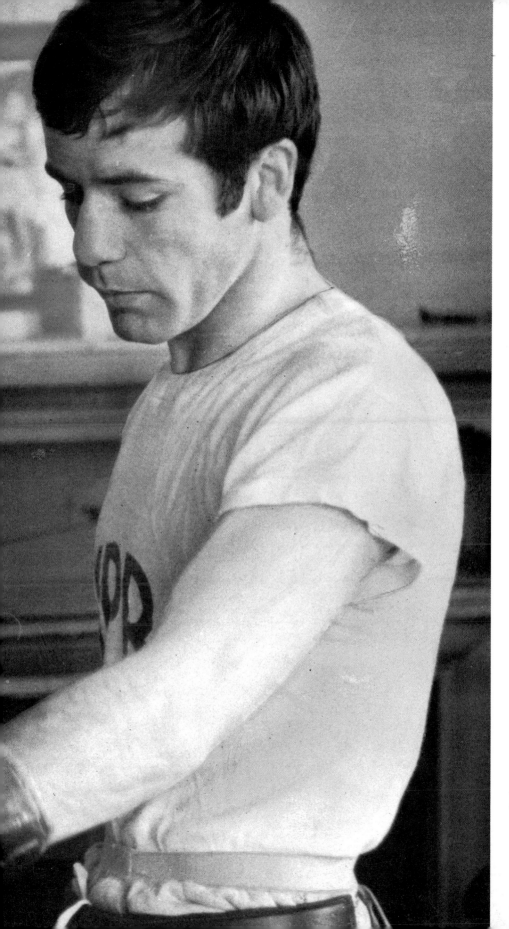

The father-and-son pairing which won a world title for Scotland, as Joe Gans prepares Walter McGowan for a sparring session.

received a badly damaged eye early in the fight. Elky bravely battled on for the full 12 rounds although many a bigger man would have quit. So bad was the injury that Elky later lost the sight of that eye. He died on 22 September 1956, his place secure as the first Scot to fight for the world flyweight title.'

And the morning after the McGowan fight the *Record* emblazoned across Page One the proud headline: 'OUR WORLD CHAMP!' The 23-year-old McGowan won on points, battling through the streaming blood of a cut eye in the latter part of the fight. The new champ said: 'I had difficulty in seeing through the blood, but after 11 rounds I knew I had only to stand up to win the title.'

At the end his father's shirt was soaked crimson red and Joe Gans, who was in his son's corner, said proudly: 'I'll never wash this shirt again. This is the proudest moment of my life.'

Rangers stars Davy Wilson, Jim Baxter and Ralph Brand congratulate Walter McGowan.

Burruni, who was ten years older than the little Scot, said: 'McGowan was too fast for me, but I think the fight should have been stopped because of his cut eyebrow.' However, the Italian's manager, Umberto Branchini, said: 'Salvatore is getting old and we are not disagreeing with the verdict.'

Promoter Jack Solomons beamed: 'I've been claiming for the last four years Walter would win a world title. Now maybe some people will listen to my predictions.'

Rangers star Jimmy Millar said, 'Walter has trained with us, and all at Ibrox, and all Scotland, are proud of him.'

At the end of the year McGowan made his first defence of the title, in far-off Bangkok, against Chartchai Chionoi. Peter Wilson cabled from Thailand: 'I doubt whether Chionoi has met anyone as fast as McGowan and, on that basis, and the fact that the Thailander has never had a 15-round bout, I am picking the Scot to retain his title, either on points, or by a stoppage late in the fight – always assuming he can avoid cuts.' But there were no tunes of glory to add to the Hogmanay revels as Wilson wrote in the last *Record* of the year in 1966:

'Brave Walter McGowan lost his world flyweight title here today with blood and tears streaming down his face. After 50 seconds of the ninth round Walter went down on his knees, tears ploughing white furrows through the scarlet mask of blood which was on his face.

'Seconds earlier Thai referee Sangwian Hiranreka had moved between the little Scot and the sinewy challenger, Chartchai Chionoi, in compassion for the truly ghastly state of the Scot's face obscured by blood from a cut across the bridge of his nose which had been pulsing gore from the second round onwards. Wee Walter was world champion no longer. And the bitter, crippling knowledge was enough to put him on the canvas, which was more than Chartchai had ever been able to do.'

The referee and one of the judges, veteran American boxing writer Nat Fleischer, had the Thai ahead on points when the fight ended. The third judge was James Sanderson, boxing writer of the *Scottish Daily Express* – the paper which at that time was the bitter main rival of the *Record*. No doubt having Sanderson as a judge didn't please the *Record*. And when he scored McGowan ahead by 39–31, Wilson delivered a magisterial rebuke: 'It was a discrepancy which I found remarkable.'

DAILY RECORD & SUNDAY MAIL

Salver of Honour

McGowan said after the fight, 'I've only lent him the title,' but sadly it was gone for ever from Walter.

There was a five-year gap before the next title glory chapter, and there was a step up in weight as well. Ken Buchanan was the new name, and the Edinburgh lightweight deserves his place in Scotland's Hall of Fame.

Buchanan was no home-town star. Instead, his major fights all took place outside Scotland – many of them in boxing's toughest backyard, the United States. He was also the first victim of the various boxing authorities who were all vying for superiority. In September 1970 he fought a wonderful battle to beat Panamanian Ismael Laguna in 90-degree heat in Puerto Rico. But the week before the fight the World Boxing Council decided to strip Laguna of his title, and the British Boxing Board of Control backed them up. It didn't matter that Buchanan was the first Briton since 1915 to win a title overseas, he didn't receive proper recognition.

That changed five months later when he out-pointed Californian Ruben Navarro in Los Angeles, and this time he *was* recognised. Navarro had been a late replacement for ex-champ Mando Ramos, who pulled out of his title chance with Buchanan three days before the fight.

Buchanan's secret sorrow was he knew he would not be able to box in his native Edinburgh. He said: 'I'd love to fight in Edinburgh as world champion more than anything in the world, but I just can't see any offers matching the money we need.'

Dick Currie, who had seen the fight at a special TV showing, praised Buchanan: 'I have rarely been so proud to be a Scot. I have watched Buchanan since he was a teenage amateur and in this Navarro fight he proved to me he was a truly great champion. He was shaken in the first round, he admits he heard "bells ringing" in his ears . . . yet he fought back to outclass his opponent.'

But if he couldn't fight in Edinburgh the citizens of Scotland's capital city were determined to pay him proper homage. Thousands cheered him when he arrived at Waverley Station and then was driven in an open-topped bus through the streets.

The mecca of boxing, Madison Square Garden, was the venue for Buchanan's defence of the title and the Scot, wearing his traditional tartan shorts, won on points against Ismael

Opposite: Triple champs: Ken Buchanan, Jim Watt and Walter McGowan meet up at a Daily Record *dinner in honour of Watt.*

Laguna. Hard-bitten New York sportswriters showered praise on Buchanan. *New York Daily News* columnist Gene Ward wrote: 'I've got news for the good folks back in Scotland . . . they have one helluva champion in the blond bomber from Edinburgh. The champion was up against a ruthless challenger but Ken Buchanan won the fight . . . won it unanimously . . . won it big.'

Larry Merchant of the *New York Post* said: 'Laguna did not come with enough to take it from Buchanan. Take it you must from a Scotsman, because he surely won't give it to you.'

Dick Currie, who was at the ringside in New York, revealed that quick thinking by manager Eddie Thomas helped save Buchanan's title bid. When challenger Laguna raised a 'mouse' under Buchanan's left eye in the third round Thomas quickly went to work. He took out a razor blade and cut a small slice in the lump, permitting the blood to run free. 'If I hadn't touched it,' Thomas explained, 'the eye might have closed completely and Ken wouldn't have been able to see out of it at all.'

Dick quoted John Condon, the top official at Madison Square Garden: 'Buchanan is a big hit here. The New York fight fans love Buchanan's honesty, his straight talking, his Scottish accent, but most of all his great skill.'

But there was no Broadway Melody of joy for Buchanan on his next visit to the Big Apple. He bit off more than he could chew when he fought the redoubtable Panamanian, Roberto Duran. Again Currie travelled to America for the fight in June 1972, to witness Buchanan lose his title when the fight was stopped in the 13th round after the referee Johny Lobianco ruled that the champion was unable to continue. Fight fans in America still talk about the bout, although Buchanan claimed later: 'Duran is just a street-fighter. He hit me with his head, his elbows, his knees and the referee didn't care.'

Dick Currie reported: 'Buchanan was totally knocked off his style by Duran's aggressive and powerful style and his street-fighting tactics. He was never allowed to get into his boxing style, using his jab and right crosses to keep off his opponent. Duran swarmed all over him, refusing to give the Scot space to move.'

The paper also spotlighted the dilemma of every fighter's wife after a defeat. It revealed that Carol Buchanan wanted her 27-year-old husband to quit boxing. She said: 'Ken phoned me and said Duran got him in the groin, but he's not sure whether it was a punch or with the knee. Yet after this low blow he could have carried on.'

The end of Buchanan's hope came in February 1975 in Tokyo and again Dick Currie made a long trip to watch Ken try to regain his world lightweight crown. But a blow which landed after the bell ended the sixth round helped him lose on points to the holder Guts Ishimatsu of Japan. It landed just below the Scot's left eye which had been damaged in a sparring accident in the week before the fight.

'I personally think Ken should retire,' wrote Currie. It was the end of Buchanan's world hopes but he was one of the most stylish of all the British champions, never mind just Scotland, who won the number-one title. How sad that eventually he fought one unlicensed bout, outwith the jurisdiction of authority.

There was a gap until April 1979 before Scotland could claim another world champion, and again it was the light-weight crown which was wrapped in tartan. 'WATT A CHAMP' hailed the *Record* on Page One of 18 April 1979. And it proudly repeated the prediction Dick Currie had made the day before that Jim Watt would win the world title around the 12th round. That's exactly what happened as he finished off Colombian Alfredo Pitalua in the 12th round at the Kelvin Hall, Glasgow, on a night drenched with emotion.

It was less than a year since Scotland's disastrous World Cup campaign in Argentina and Alex Cameron wrote of Watt: 'He has become an instant folk hero to erase from memory the suffering of Argentina.'

Watt, from Moodiesburn near Glasgow, praised the fans: 'No one will ever know how much I owe them. They relaxed me when I needed it, they encouraged me when I needed it and I can tell them now it's my aim to have any future world title fight in front of these same people.'

He was as good as his word. The 31-year-old was back at the Kelvin Hall on 9 November of the same year to hammer American Robert Vasquez into submission in the ninth round, even though his opponent was ten years younger. Dick Currie wrote: 'Vasquez found the champion too good and the occasion too big.' But Watt had made sure it was a one-sided fight.

Watt certainly kept busy. He was in action again at the Kelvin Hall the following March, with a stunning win against

Jim Watt wins the European Championship, beating Frenchman André Holyk in 1 minute 42 seconds.

Irish challenger Charlie Nash when the fight was stopped in the fourth round. Currie described the victory: 'Jim Watt retained his title like a true champion. The London referee, Syd Nathan, had no alternative but to take a bemused, bewildered Irish challenger back to his corner after his third knockdown.'

Watt moved venues, but it was still Glasgow that staged the next fight – an open-air Saturday night title clash at Ibrox Stadium against American Howard Davis. The title-holder won on points over 15 rounds and Dick Currie wrote: 'Jim Watt is the best lightweight in the world. Make no mistake about that. The proof was there for all to see at Ibrox Park on Saturday night. Scotland's Prince of Punch was too good for American Howard Davis, the man who claimed he would take home Watt's world title.'

Watt ended 1980 with yet another defence back at the Kelvin Hall, this time in the early hours of the morning so that the fight could be seen on American prime-time TV. The referee stopped the contest against Irish-American Sean O'Grady in the twelfth round in a bloodbath of a fight which had the challenger's father, Pat, claiming: 'I have protested to WBC president Jose Sulaiman over the incident.'

But Watt, who had five world-title wins to his credit, said: 'There's no way I deliberately used the head on O'Grady.' Watt later joked: 'Somebody asked me about fighting at three o'clock in the morning, and I said, "Everyone in Glasgow fights at three o'clock in the morning."'

Defeat came for Watt eventually, as it invariably comes for all champions, on a Saturday night at Wembley in June 1980, when he lost on points to Nicaraguan Alexis Arguello.

Jim Watt prepares for a world title fight watched by manager Terry Lawless (centre) and the Record's *boxing writer, Dick Currie (second left).*

As he prepared for retirement, Watt revealed: 'My family can't be expected to go on taking second place to boxing. I thought I would be in tears when I lost the title. In a strange way I felt relief. I've hardly had any life outside the gym and I'm a man who loves his family and a bit of golf. People are fed up with moans in defeat and I made up my mind I wouldn't do that despite my disappointment.'

Watt has gone on to become an articulate and respected TV pundit on boxing in a career that has been as impressive as his world title reign.

It wasn't until 1992 that Scotland could hail their next champion, when Pat Clinton from the little village of Croy won the world flyweight title. This was the WBO version – by this time boxing was almost choking on alphabet soup with so many governing bodies all organising world fights at every level.

Champion line-up: world flyweight title-holder Pat Clinton (centre) with former Olympic champ Dick McTaggart (left) and ex-world champion Walter McGowan.

It was at Jim Watt's favourite arena, the Kelvin Hall, that Clinton beat Mexican holder Isidro 'Sid' Perez on points: 'a nail-biting decision,' according to Dick Currie. The *Record*'s boxing writer added: 'I hate to be a spoilsport, but I had Perez in front by one round. Still, the former British and European champion deserved his break after a gallant show.' The 27-year-old Clinton took the title on the verdicts of the two American judges, the Danish referee giving it to Perez.

Six months later, in September 1992, Clinton successfully defended his title in the Scottish Exhibition Centre in Glasgow, with a points verdict over Danny Porter. It provoked controversy, and even boos at the end of the fight. Jim Watt later told Alex Cameron in the *Record*: 'I was disappointed in Clinton, but he did enough to win.' Watt went on: 'I'd love to have given the decision to wee Danny Porter because at least he wanted to fight.'

In May 1993, Clinton's short reign as world king ended when he lost to South Africa's Baby Jake Matlala, again in the SECC, when he suffered his first knock-out and the referee stopped the fight in the eighth round. Baby Jake, at 4ft 10in, floored Clinton three times in the eighth to finish off the Scot's spell as world champion. A come-back at bantamweight proved unsuccessful.

These were the men who became Scotland's world champions but, like Elky Clark in the 1920s, three others fought unsuccessfully for the crown.

Tommy Milligan lost a world middleweight fight in London on 30 June 1927 to the American champion Mickey Walker, and the Scot's defeat in the tenth round was front-page news.

Then, in January 1952, Peter Keenan – one of the most famous boxing Scots not to win a world title – lost his chance of the world bantamweight title when he was beaten on points by Vic Toweel of South Africa in Johannesburg.

Chic Calderwood lost a world light heavyweight clash to the Puerto Rican holder, Jose Torres, in San Juan in October 1966. The Scot was knocked out in the second round. Sadly, only a month after his world championship attempt, Calderwood was killed in a car crash back in Scotland.

There has been gloom as well as glory for so many of Scotland's fight stars. But whatever happened outside the ring,

Previous page: The joy of victory: Pat Clinton retains his WBO flyweight title against Londoner Danny Porter in September 1992.

with unsuccessful battles against weight, the bottle or gambling, nothing can take away from the great moments inside it. If only briefly they made generations of Scots feel on top of the world, these memories mustn't be diminished.

Grand Slam Victors

Rugby's Amateur Tradition

For most of the past hundred years, Scottish rugby rolled along in its own little world, drawing its main support from middle-class enclaves in the big cities and the fiercely partisan strongholds of the Borders, where it is the universal sport.

There was no domination of the sporting scene similar to the way rugby ruled in Wales. Indeed, the exact opposite took place in Scotland, where in popular terms it existed well behind soccer in the public interest. But the times they are a-changing. Now we see massive multi-million-pound TV deals, World Cups with wall-to-wall coverage, players writing newspaper columns, a transfer system in all but name, and Scotland's captain Gavin Hastings as well known as Gary McAllister, the skipper of the international soccer team.

All this would most certainly have been frowned on by J. Aikman Smith, the formidable secretary of the Scottish Rugby Union between the wars. When King George V asked him why the Scotland international side did not have numbers on their backs Smith is reported to have replied, 'It's a match, not a cattle sale.' Indeed, the poor old King didn't live to see those numbers as he died early in 1936, the year they were finally introduced.

The SRU were a beacon of sporting conservatism. So keen were they to maintain a simon-pure amateurism in the nasty real world, they fell over into ridicule. When Jock Wemyss played for Scotland after the First World War (in which he had lost an eye) he was charged 7s 6d (37½p) for a jersey it was claimed he had not returned after a pre-war international.

The Scots criticised intensely the New Zealand Union, who had made daily expenses payments to players on the 1905 tour of Britain, and a rift developed which lasted nearly 30 years. Relations were so bad that the touring All Blacks in 1924–25 did not play in Scotland, and fans were denied the chance of seeing the team dubbed 'The Invincibles' who won all 28 matches in their tour of the rest of the British Isles.

The famous New Zealand writer Terry McLean said as recently as 1981 that 'Administration has not been Scotland's greatest contribution to rugby. The attitude towards amateurism has amounted to a fetish. That great-hearted man, Bill Dickinson, who coached the team in 1975 and many other Scottish sides, was thrown off a team bus in 1978 because he had appeared on a TV programme about rugger.'

And yet the keepers of the flame of total amateurism had a professional attitude in other directions. They had the foresight to build Murrayfield to give Scotland's international team a proper home, and the magnificent stadium's name is renowned throughout the sporting world. They were also, even in the Edwardian era, willing to take chances with players. Can you imagine the publicity today if Scotland's selectors followed the example of those far-off days and picked a player for the international team who was still at school? K.G. MacLeod of Fettes College was just 17 when he was picked as centre against New Zealand in 1905. He then went on to win nine more caps when he was at Cambridge University, before he retired at the ripe old age of 21. He later captained Lancashire at cricket, played football for Manchester City and won an amateur golf title in South Africa.

However, two decades after MacLeod's debut is really the foundation of modern rugby in Scotland. On 21 March 1925 Murrayfield was opened and, like a chapter out of a sporting novel, it was marked by Scotland winning their first-ever

Grand Slam, victories in the international championship against France, Ireland, Wales and England.

The *Record* on the following Monday morning hailed it with a whole page, topped off with four rows of headlines in the small type of the time. The sub-editors wrapped it in a tartan theme with a strap line: 'Rugger Scots Wha Hae Won Championship and Calcutta Cup'. That was followed by the main heading: 'Auld Scotia's Champion Sons', and a cluster of sub-headings: 'Saxons fall in memorable struggle before record crowd at Murrayfield – well-matched sides' and the final message in a typographical hotch-potch: 'England's final fiery rally fails – every Scot pulls his weight – a glorious victory'.

Scotland had won 14–11, to add to the 25–4 victory over France in the last international played at the old ground at Inverleith. They then beat Wales 24–14 in Swansea and the attacking star of both these matches was 'The Flying Scotsman', Ian Smith, on the left wing, who scored an amazing eight tries in two internationals.

Scotland won 14–8 in Dublin and the stage was set for Murrayfield. The side contained such legendary names as Dan Drysdale at full-back, half-backs Herbert Waddell and J.B. Nelson, and John Bannerman in the pack. It was a victory hailed throughout the world, the only unhappy people being some of the fans who attended that opening day at Murrayfield, and who had been caught in crowd congestion. The *Record*, then as now always on the side of the fan, reported:

'Murrayfield is undoubtedly a fine ground; it appears to be all that has been claimed for it. The Scottish Rugby Football Union, however, might show a little more consideration for the public which supplies them with funds. Of course that is an old story – and an old sore.

'One of the unfortunates on Saturday who got stuck in the narrow bottle-neck leading to the entrance to the ground, and did not get inside until the teams were just turning out, naturally thinks the Union should do something. By that time it was impossible to see anything from the top of the banking, where the spectators were lined four or five deep.

'He tried several times but could not even see the field. At last, however, with others, when one of the enclosure entrances was opened, he managed to gain a position from which he could see about three-fourths of the field. The remaining part was entirely hidden by the stand.

'What amazed him, though, was to observe there were quite a number of gaps. Judicious packing would have enabled hundreds more to have seen the game in comfort, and would have saved an immense amount of grumbling.

'If the getting into the ground was difficult, the getting away from it was worse. It was really amazing to learn that there were no accidents, so severe was the crush. There are hundreds, if not thousands, who despite the result found the first game at Murrayfield anything but pleasant.'

The crowd was reported to be 60,000, and 'Gaberlunzie', reporting the game, concentrated more on the win against England than the Grand Slam:

'The opening of Murrayfield will be memorable on account of a victory over England. It is even more satisfactory in that a long history of English wins in Scotland, stretching back to 1912, has at last been broken.

'The continuance of that run of success would not have been to the good of the game. From all points of view, even in English interests, the result therefore was altogether to the good. Scotland, as champions, took possession of the Calcutta Cup.

'I have seen many finer exhibitions of high-class football in an international, but not many in which the sides were so evenly matched.'

Gaberlunzie wasn't too happy with the press-box. He said sniffily: 'From the elevated position of the press seats it was often difficult to identify players. In the heat of the last ten minutes the man who brought down Corbett from behind after he had passed Drysdale and was about to step over the line, saved the match for Scotland.'

Unfortunately, the readers have yet to be told who this heroic defender was. The match was so close that Scotland were 10–11 down with twenty minutes to play. But after more Scottish pressure the winning move was described: 'Aitken, in carrying on with his feet, drove the ball against a post with a sure try in sight, but from the ensuing scrummage Waddell set himself up for a drop, and Nelson played up to him. So

Scotland led by 14 points to 11 and it remained at that.'

The heroes of the roaring '20s were: D. Drysdale (Heriot's FPs); A.C. Wallace, G.G. Aitken, G.P.S. McPherson and I.S. Smith (Oxford University); H. Waddell and J.B. Nelson (Glasgow Academicals); J.M. Bannerman, J.C.H. Ireland (Glasgow High School FPs) J.W. Scott (Stewart's College), D.S. Davies (Hawick), D.J. MacMyn (Cambridge University), R.H. Howie (Kirkcaldy), J.R. Paterson (Birkenhead Park), A.C. Gillies (Watsonians).

Scotland won the Triple Crown twice before the start of the Second World War, in 1933 and 1938. The Grand Slam was no longer available, because the home countries pulled out of matches with France after the 1930–31 season after a row with their Federation.

But it was the 1938 triumph which etched itself into history. It depended on the final match, against England at Twickenham – the first-ever Calcutta Cup match to be tele-vised. Not that there were any viewers north of the border as TV didn't start in Scotland for another 13 years.

The match is remembered for one man's display. The Scotland captain was hailed in a *Record* headline on Monday, 21 March 1938: 'Wilson Shaw, with best-ever display, silences critics.' The Glasgow High School FP scored two tries in a 21–16 victory for Scotland. This time the writer's nom-de-plume was 'Rugger' and he started: 'What a setting for this diamond jubilee match and what a game.' He went on: 'Neither Twickenham, bathed in sunshine and packed with 70,000, nor any other ground has witnessed a more gripping contest than this, which saw Scotland achieve her three-fold aim of championship, Calcutta Cup and Triple Crown.' He paid tribute to the captain and described the try that sealed victory:

'Wilson Shaw set the seal on a brilliant display with a daz-zling try. Taking a beautiful pass from Dorward, he sold a dummy to Reynolds and went right through at terrific speed to beat Parker and Unwin for pace and threw himself over at the corner.

'The roar which greeted this might have been heard in the centre of Glasgow, and it was repeated the next minute when Shaw fielded the restarting kick, sent it into touch and the referee blew his final blast.'

Shaw was carried shoulder-high from the pitch, as

Scotland rejoiced at the victory.

That was a result to be remembered with a warm glow, rather like the after-effects of a malt whisky. Not so the score from a glamour game after the war when the touring Springboks visited Murrayfield in November 1951. It was arguably the blackest day for Scottish rugby as South Africa won 44–0. Hugh Young, who had started a long, distinguished stint as the paper's writer, praised the South Africans:

'What a wonderful performance they put up. Here was a lesson that will be quoted for years to come. No team in the world would have been ashamed to have been beaten by such a combination.

'But there was no need for our side to allow the score to mount to such a fantastic total despite the crushing superiority of the tourists. Our defence was non-existent and the only man who seemed to have the least idea of the proper way to tackle was W.I.D. Elliot. This was Elliot's 21st international. He has never had to work harder and he did his work well. A pack of Elliots might have given us a more respectable score.'

Hugh Young, and the rest of Scottish rugby, had a long wait until there was a Grand Slam triumph to equal that of 1925. Matches with France were resumed after the war, and although there were many games which were individual triumphs, Scotland couldn't string them together to take the biggest prize of them all.

Then in 1984 it all came right at last. Wins against Wales in Cardiff, England at Murrayfield and Ireland in Dublin set up a decider against France at Murrayfield. Hugh Young's match preview began:

'The Grand Slam birthday party to crown them all – that's the target for 15 Scots who can become legends at Murrayfield this afternoon. Sixty thousand fanatical fans in the ground and millions watching on TV will be willing Scotland to crush flamboyant France and write coach Jim Telfer's 44th birthday into the history books.

'I say they will do just that. The players are ready to end an agonising 59-year wait and lay the ghosts of the 1925 squad, the only Scottish team to nail the Slam. Led by 36-year-old veteran, Jim Aitken, they'll do it for the glory and for the man they idolise – Jim Telfer. The man they call the Lion has transformed a bunch of also-rans

Opposite: All-time greats: Scotland full-backs Andy Irvine (left) and Gavin Hastings, snapped together in 1983.

139

into a triumphant Triple Crown machine.'

As history beckoned, skipper Jim Aitken said, 'There's no point in getting our knickers in a twist. We've tackled each game on its merits and that's got to be the thinking again.'

Rugby had shaken off some of its cobwebs. The players had their first names listed instead of just their initials, and they even talked to the press. The line-up was Peter Dods; Jim Pollock, Keith Robertson, David Johnston, Roger Baird; John Rutherford, Roy Laidlaw; Jim Aitken, Colin Deans, Ian Milne, Alister Campbell, Alan Tomes, Jim Calder, Ian Paxton, David Leslie.

The back page of the paper was given over to the match, with a picture of Milne, Deans and Aitken under the headline 'LE CRUNCH', and a subheading 'Front-line furies set to roar'. And so they did, as the paper went crazy on Monday,

19 March 1984. Hugh Young put the spotlight on one player: 'Looking as though he had gone 15 rounds with the heavyweight champion of the world, full-back Peter Dods still managed a smile as he came off the Murrayfield pitch. No wonder. The Border joiner had scored 17 of Scotland's points in their 21–12 Grand Slam victory over the frustrated French. In doing so, quietly-spoken Dods smashed the record number of points in a Scottish championship season. The legendary Andy Irvine had held it with 35 points. Dods extended that figure to a round 50 for this season's campaign.

'When I congratulated him, Dods said, "Record? I'd forgotten all about it. But thanks." His black eye, which brought gasps of concern from TV viewers all round the world, was caused in the early stages by a knee. Peering

A superb try for Gavin Hastings against France, 1988.

Right in the thick of things, John Jeffrey clashes with the Welsh, and everybody seems to have forgotten about the ball.

through the puffed-up flesh surrounding his right eye, Dods dismissed it all lightly. "My eye watered for a bit but it soon settled down and it didn't interrupt my vision."

'If Dods was the spectacular points-gatherer, it was one of the normally unsung heroes of the pack who brought a special mention from Scots coach Jim Telfer. Breaking a long-held tradition, Telfer said, "I don't usually single-out players. But I thought prop Iain Milne had a magnificent game. He out-scrummaged his opponent and he held our pack together with his sheer strength and skill. I've given Iain a lot of stick over the years but he's never complained and I thought he was outstanding."'

Alex Cameron switched press-boxes to join in the celebrations.

'What a pity Scotland's World Cup prima donnas could not have been sent to Murrayfield to see the wonders of the will to win. Here were great Scots, outplayed and apparently heading for the mincer, who turned the match round and into Grand Slam history. Could Jock Stein's well-heeled professionals perform such a feat of endeavour against a superior side, schooled in a higher standard of club games? On current form, the answer is definitely No.'

The centre pages were given over to the celebrations and the paper revealed under a giant 'Saturday night fever' head-line:

'It was, after all, one of those nights. And Scotland's greats weren't going to be left out of it as Edinburgh went wild. The black-tied, black-eyed heroes slipped out to join jubilant fans in a pub off Princes Street for a quick pint and a sing-song *before* the official reception. And in the Guildford Arms, surrounded by a scrum of cheering Scots, they celebrated in style a historic occasion: Scotland's first Grand Slam for 59 years.

Gavin Hastings and Kenny Milne.

'Then, shepherded by captain Jim Aitken, it was back to the banquet, as the fans toasted a famous victory. Douce old Edinburgh hadn't seen anything like it. The champagne flowed like lager, the lager like water. The whisky took care of itself. And Saturday night fever really took over the capital's centre.

'Yesterday Roy Laidlaw, the man who was a key player in Scotland's success, nursed a pint of lager instead of a morning coffee and explained their pub jaunt: "It's traditional to go there after an international. We were only in for about 15 minutes, and we bought our own pints. It was great. We were chatting to the fans and belting out 'Flower of Scotland'. Jim got us back to the hotel for the banquet and the dance. I got to my bed about 2.30. I was very, very tired."'

There was a giant picture of a bow-tied Iain Milne clutching a pint, with his arm round two pretty girls caught in a bigger scrum than there had been earlier at Murrayfield. Fittingly, the last word on the game went to Herbert Waddell, who played in the 1925 Grand Slam side: 'Terrific', and the *Record* echoed him: 'All Scotland would go along with that.'

Mercifully, the wait for the next Grand Slam wasn't as long. This time it was a mere six years and the boys of the old brigade were together in a fascinating feature as a build-up to the 1990 game. Jack Adams reunited two heroes of the past:

'They are the Grandest Grand Slammers of them all – the two surviving members of the first Scotland side to sweep the board clean in 1925. It was a privilege to reunite 92-years-young Bob Howie and Jimmy Ireland, six years his junior, in the week of Scotland's bid for Slam No. 3 against England at Murrayfield on Saturday. This partnership was at the hub of that first clean sweep which made Murrayfield's first international all those years ago so extra special.

'Jimmy, hooker in those days, is still steeped in the game and has since been international referee, president of the SRU and is now unofficial historian for Murrayfield. "I still go to games, especially GHK's home games, as I am an honorary president. But it's a different game. There have been too many changes to the rules in a bid to speed up the game and make it more open for the spectators. Sadly the changes have had the opposite effect."

'Jimmy's prop was tough Kirkcaldy farmer, Bob Howie. He said: "I won't be there on Saturday. I have lost a bit of interest. It is just a bashing game now. The first SRU handbook I was given with the laws was pretty thin; now it's as thick as a bible. It would take one of these computer things to referee a game now."

'Jimmy Ireland recalled: "If you were honoured with an international jersey then you were expected to wear it for your whole career. I stupidly swapped mine after a game and had to fork out 12s 6d (62½p) to the SRU to buy a new one."

'Both showed their Old Corinthian upbringing when photographer Eric Craig asked them to pose with a new ball. With only a look passing between them, they turned it to hide the maker's name. Jimmy said, "That sort of thing isn't for us. The more money coming into the game, the more sportsmanship goes out of it. We never bothered about anything else except beating England."'

This time the final game was the one every fan wanted, against England at Murrayfield. Jack Adams previewed the match:

'England must finally reveal the truth against Scotland this afternoon – are they magic or just another myth?

'And, while England have everything to prove, Scotland have only to show over these 80 minutes that they are better than England. I reckon they are. It's the first time ever the auld enemies have met in their final game with *both* unbeaten. That means the Calcutta Cup, Triple Crown and Grand Slam are all up for grabs at Murrayfield – a fitting finale to the real clash between the bruisers and the cruisers.

'Scotland have had to sweat for their wins over Ireland, France and Wales. Each game has been a battle. England, on the other hand, have been able to ramble through their games. Now it's the day of the bruisers, when the going gets tough and our battle-hardened toughs get going.'

Colin Price, writer for the *Record*'s sister paper, the *Daily Mirror*, put his English viewpoint – which highlighted their view they would win easily – and it turned out to be one of those fatal mistakes in the history of international rugby.

'England will put the bite on White Shark John Jeffrey

Princess Anne, patron of the Scottish Rugby Union, has really made captain David Sole smile before a World Cup fixture.

John Jeffrey looks certain to win this ball against England.

Dash for freedom, as Scotland scrum-half Gary Armstrong tries to set up an attack against Japan in the World Cup.

Flying Scot Gary Armstrong wins the ball as Scotland stalwart John Jeffrey watches with concern.

and his Scots piranhas, and send a chill down the spines of the mighty All Blacks,' he crowed. 'For all the boiling Scots passion in this unique winner-takes-all showdown, I see only one winner in Murrayfield's searing cauldron.'

The men chosen to make Adams' prediction come true on Saturday, 17 March 1990, were Gavin Hastings; Tony Stanger, Scott Hastings, Sean Lineen, Iwan Tukalo; Craig Chalmers, Gary Armstrong; David Sole, Kenny Milne, Paul Burnell, Chris Gray, Damian Cronin, John Jeffrey, Derek White, Finlay Calder.

The paper helpfully printed two verses of 'Flower of Scotland', which had become so much the Murrayfield anthem that even the Princess Royal, patron of the SRU and a regular attender at internationals, was seen to sing it.

Jack Adams triumphantly started his Monday morning match report on the 13–7 victory:

'Well, if that is what two verses can do, just wait till we learn the whole song.

'The magic of Murrayfield will linger a long, long time. We won the Calcutta Cup, the Triple Crown, the Five Nations Championship and the Grand Slam. And England were sent homewards with really only the poll tax left to think about. The first 10 minutes are seared into my memory for ever. Everything that moved, spoke with an English accent or even looked slightly strange was hammered into the deck.

'This was Bannockburn with our boots on and after that torrid start England were well and truly rucked. They could have been a good team, a very good team if we had let them off the hook. This was a real team effort and we can carve their names with pride. Gavin Hastings, so big and strong and yet so deft. That kick ahead which sent Tony Stanger clear for his try at the start of the second half was marvellous.

'Stanger, Scott Hastings, Sean Patrick Lineen and Iwan Tukalo were tigers in the tackle, the men who would not be moved. At half-back, Craig Chalmers, with three superb penalties, carved out the headstone for England's boastful hopes. Gary Armstrong, for me, was man of the match – all guts and courage as he turned Murrayfield into his own private preserve. Then those forwards. What a riot they were as they hammered home a lesson in humility to the English in scrum, ruck and maul. Oh, what flower power.

'Even a superbly worked English try couldn't floor us. When Jeremy Guscott sold such a perfect dummy that half the terracing was going along Princes Street the wrong way, it gave us a helluva fright – but nothing more.

'With the injured Derek White replaced by Derek Turnbull, Scotland had to change their back row, but not their ambition. The fact that England had opportunities to kick penalties but decided instead to scrummage says more for their insolence than their intelligence. Perhaps now England will realise that these games are won with the heart – not the mouth.'

Adams was certainly the busiest journalist in Scotland that weekend. He also conducted the paper's immensely popular Sports Hotline, where readers phone in their views. In fine fettle, Jack started:

'Hang down your head, Bill Beaumont, hang down your head in shame. BBB – Big Biased Bill – has certainly got up your sporrans. It's all because the commentator was less than graceful in his acceptance of the fact that England were lucky to come second at Murrayfield. For those of you who might have spent the weekend potholing or just hiding from the mother-in-law, the fact is that Scotland's team not only had the damned cheek to turn up to play the might of England, the rotters even beat them!

'Bill Beaumont's TV comments were certainly not the flavour of the month with Hotline callers. Jonathan Miller, from East Kilbride, said: "Congratulations to Scotland. They certainly did us all proud. Bill Beaumont has quickly taken over from Jimmy Hill as the most hated Englishman in Scotland. It obviously hurt him to pay any tribute to the Scots. I am really glad our boys sent him homeward to think again."

'And Jack Hume, Edinburgh, called to say: "According to Beaumont the referee was biased, the wind was blowing the wrong way and it was too dry a day. What a sad excuse for a commentator."'

Under the heading 'Upon my Sole', the ever-busy Jack popped up on the back page. Scotland were leaving for New Zealand shortly after the England game and coach Ian

Unrestrained joy greets an historic win over England.

Hats off to the new Murrayfield. Scotland international brothers, Gavin and Scott Hastings (right) examine the rebuilt stadium.

McGeechan, the architect of the victory, said, 'Maybe now the New Zealanders will take us seriously. This really is a tremendous squad. They have done Scotland proud. And on behalf of everyone I want to thank the fans. The atmosphere at Murrayfield was unbelievable.'

Just in case there was anywhere in the paper readers missed that wee man Adams' name, he also provided the words on the centre pages, revealing how the squad dressed up in kilts, and fancy shirts, for the after-match banquet:

'Oh, what a night it was for Scotland's 15 newest folk-heroes. They really let it rip after their historic Grand Slam win, over England at Murrayfield. There was not a dry eye in the place, but there were certainly plenty of wet glasses. Resplendent in their Highland dress, these lads were definitely the Flowers of Scotland – until they removed their jackets to display a nightmare of shirts. It had all to do with a bet on who could sport the most outrageous shirt beneath his formal gear. Iwan Tukalo got my vote for his horrible Paisley-patterned effort but, as the night wore on, the identity of the actual winner became less clear and just as less relevant.

'And there to pay tribute was soccer star Ally McCoist, who joined the Scotland team for the after-match party. He missed Rangers' game against St Mirren because of injury, but that didn't stop him joining the flower power brigade at Murrayfield – and a few other watering holes. "These guys are really something special. They are what sport is all about, and did the whole nation proud. But imagine if they ever start kissing each other when they scored – it would be a horror movie," he said.'

Scotland's supporters are used to the swings in the international side's fortunes. However, the reshaped Murrayfield was not celebrated in the same way as 1925, with a Grand Slam win. By any standards season 1993–94 was something short of ordinary, with a punishing 51–15 defeat from the All Blacks – maybe the SRU should have found some reason not to play them again – and not one win in the Five Nations Championship. But some time in the future Scotland will put together another Grand Slam side, and hopefully the gap will not be as long as the 59 years between 1925 and 1984.

Rugby, next to boxing, faces the most uncertain future of any sport. Not because of any threat to its existence, but

Previous page: Iwan Tukalo powers past Ireland.

because of doubts about the structure of the sport. Huge gate receipts and TV fees for internationals are generated, and players are asked to devote more and more time to the game. I await with interest the formula the game's administration devises, instead of the tinkering with the problems that has taken place so far.

Will we see the day when rugby transfers take over from football deals on the back page? That would be a world which Aikman Smith, the secretary of those far-off interwar years, would have never imagined in his wildest nightmares. But it may not be far from becoming reality.

Kings of Europe!

Celtic, Rangers and Aberdeen

Celtic's victory in the European Cup final in 1967 was the greatest in the history of Scottish football. Their 2–1 win against Inter Milan, giants of Italian football, made them not just the first British side to win the European Cup, but the first non-Latin team.

No other Scottish team, either club or international, has achieved such a result at such a level. The Celtic team were dubbed the Lisbon Lions, and they marched into history with more battle honours than even the famous Scottish regiments, having taken the League Championship, Scottish Cup, League Cup and Glasgow Cup. These achievements in season 1966–67 when they won every tournament they entered were rightly lauded, but success in their own backyard would not alone have put Celtic on such an exalted pedestal.

It was holding up the top prize in Europe that made Celtic so special, and they were proudly followed by Rangers winning the Cup-Winners' Cup in 1972 and Aberdeen who captured the same trophy 11 years after it had been at Ibrox.

'John, you're immortal!' bellowed the irrepressible

The proudest manager in Europe: Jock Stein in his Parkhead office with the European Cup sitting on his desk, 1967.

Liverpool manager Bill Shankly to Celtic boss Jock Stein in the dressing-room at the end of the European Cup final in Lisbon's sun-soaked National Stadium. Sadly Stein, by then Scotland manager, died in 1985 but wily old Shankly was right: the memory of Stein and the players he led that afternoon in Lisbon is immortal.

Here's how the *Record* reported that match in a million in a May week in 1967. The paper didn't neglect the amazing

Jock Stein and that Cup:
This time the Celtic boss is
showing off the European
trophy to some of Scotland's
referees at their 1967
summer conference. Jack
Mowat, chief referee
supervisor, is front right.

army of 10,000 Celtic fans who had travelled to Portugal. Donald Bruce didn't miss out any colour as he reported:

'Lisbon, sweltering city of a million twinkling lights under a pale yellow moon, tonight belongs to Glasgow. The city, which has seen many sights, has never witnessed anything quite like this before. They flew in, and Lisbon's airport described the extra flights – about 30 – as "slightly chaotic". That was possibly the understatement of the year.

'They motored in, some on two cylinders. They hiked on both feet. John McCarroll of Croy, for instance, has been on the hitch-hike road since 12 May. He arrived here this afternoon, with the wearing of the green.

'But hail! hail! The Celts (and their fans) are here. Tonight they have taken over the bars of this beautiful city – and it's extraordinary how the names of the more notorious ones seem to be world known. The Union Jack flutters bravely in the breeze over the British Embassy in Lisbon's San Domingo Street, but inside the stiff upper-lip trembles slightly. A British Embassy official said: "We are slightly apprehensive. I think some of us will take to the hills until the match is over."

'Like every other Scot here I am wearing a Celtic

badge tonight. When I told Jock Stein it was the first time I had ever worn one, he said: "You should be proud to wear it." I hope to be even prouder tomorrow night.'

The ebullient Hugh Taylor detailed Celtic's march through Europe in his inimitable style, starting with their first-round tie against Swiss side Zurich of whom he said, 'They were expected to be as meek and mild as condensed milk but they turned out to be as bleak and formidable as an Alp with a hangover.'

Then it was Nantes, where he remembered the town's mayor using a speech of welcome to Celtic to criticise the French President, Charles De Gaulle. He reported he went back a hundred years in time watching peasants toil in the drab countryside outside Novi Sad, when Celtic went to Yugoslavia to play Vojvodina.

But there was nothing drab about Celtic's dramatic last-gasp winner from skipper Billy McNeill against the Yugoslavs at Parkhead. Remember this was in the era before colour TV, and Taylor said: 'This was the goal I said should be filmed in Technicolor, the most exciting I've seen in the European Cup.' Then came the semi-final win against Dukla Prague of Czechoslovakia, and it was on to Lisbon.

Few managers nowadays announce their teams for even minor matches before the kick-off. They seem to imagine opponents tremble and lie awake gnawed with nerves wondering who they will play against. Jock Stein would have none of such managerial nonsense. He flew into Lisbon and announced his line-up two days before the match: Simpson, Craig, Gemmell, Murdoch, McNeill, Clark, Johnstone, Wallace, Chalmers, Auld, Lennox. I wonder if they could have really believed the place in Scotland's football history that waited for them.

No details were missed out in the paper, which found a corner to record that 'Celtic left Scotland well supplied with food. They took with them 70 Aberdeen-Angus steaks, 30 spring lamb chops from Perthshire-fed sheep, 10lb of gammon and 10lb of sausages. They also packed 18 loaves, 12lb of Scotch tomatoes and an ample supply of tea. That lot should be enough to see them through till Thursday.'

Opponents Inter Milan were hit a hammerblow when manager Helenio Herrera announced that key man Luis Suarez would not play. He was injured and had not even travelled to Portugal. Right to the kick-off, though, Stein believed the Italians would fly in Suarez.

The *Record* itself had not yet made history as the first major British paper to be printed in colour. So in its biggest type, 144-point thin face, white on a black border, it proclaimed on the main sports page the simple message: 'CHAMPIONS OF EUROPE'.

Hugh Taylor detailed how the Italians had gone ahead from a penalty in seven minutes, scored by Sandro Mazzola. He described how Celtic had hit back and Inter kept them at bay:

'The luckiest defence in the world held out. Then Tommy Gemmell struck. What a great goal it was and it shows you how much in command Celtic were that it was made by right-back Jim Craig.

'Gemmell to Craig and back, and what a shot from Tommy. His first-time right-foot shot thundered into the back of the net like a flash. The great Sarti was beaten and the exotic stadium turned into a green and white inferno. The Inter players knew in their hearts this was the end, the end of a once-great team.

'It was only a matter of time before Celtic got the winner. Anxiety set in, however, as the minutes ticked away and the winner Celtic deserved did not come. With only five minutes to go Celtic scored the goal that made history – the goal that made them the first British club to win the European Cup.

'Bobby Murdoch was the man behind it. In yet another fast and fascinating attack Inter's defence was ripped apart and Bobby slammed in a low, hard, angular drive. As Sarti moved to cover it Stevie Chalmers stuck out a foot to deflect the ball into the net.

'Be proud of Celtic. This was history and what terrific history it was. I think only Super Celts could have come back from such a disastrous start – a start that would have knocked practically every other team in Europe out the ring. But not Celtic. They played all the better, all the harder. And they were entitled to call themselves great champions, for great champions they were.

'It would have been the tragedy of all time if Inter had won the Cup. For they took the lashing of a lifetime. This was no cool contemptuous defence. This was Inter

Stevie Wonder: striker Steve Chalmers steers the ball home past helpless Inter Milan keeper Sarti for the winning goal in the 1967 European Cup.

at panic stations. This was Inter meeting much more than their match.

'It was a defeat at last for the method men of Inter to whom defence is law. It was a game packed with drama, incident and excitement, and it all came from Celtic.'

The *Record* reported the chaos that followed the victory as thousands of Celtic fans swept on to the pitch at the National Stadium:

'Billy McNeill, Celtic's magnificent European Cup skipper, found his glory night ending in fear. For McNeill had to fight his way through the joy-crazed Celtic fans to reach the presentation dais. He said afterwards: "It was the most frightening thing I've known. I realised at the end of the game that I could not go to receive the Cup because of the field invasion. But they came to the dressing-room for me. It was terrible trying to fight our way through the crowds to the other side of the stadium. Luckily they realised that I could not go back the same

way. A police car was laid on to take me round the outside of the stadium to the dressing-rooms . . . just me and the Cup!'"

The paper described the ordeal for some of the other Celtic players who, it said, took knocks and bruises as they left the field:

'One Portuguese fan tried to rip off Bertie Auld's jersey. The inside-left was thrown to the ground by fans and police had to rescue him. Tommy Gemmell had his jersey torn before he could exchange it with one of the Inter players. The Portuguese police could do nothing to stop the Scots. The lush turf of the National Stadium was cut up and taken away as souvenirs. The centre spot did not exist at all when the fans had cleared the park.'

Page One that morning, 26 May 1967, was cleared for a huge picture of Jock Stein and Bobby Murdoch holding the European Cup and the headline proclaimed: 'CELTIC V-E NIGHT '67!' And in the leader column the paper hailed Stein:

We've won the Cup! And it's party time for Celtic's squad after the 1967 European Cup triumph in Lisbon.

161

'Today he's the uncrowned king of Scotland. And if the Scottish Nationalists ever get their way he'll be a front-runner for President of the Scottish Free State. For Jock Stein is the man who, with his magnificent team for whom no praise can be too lavish, has put Scottish football right back where it belongs. Bang at the top!

'There's not a football fan in all Britain this morning – no matter his allegiance – who will begrudge the cheers the Celtic team and their very great manager have so wonderfully earned. And remembering the honours bestowed on England when they won the World Cup – and were trounced by Scotland – it's fair to ask two questions this very happy morning. Whaur's yer Sir Alf Ramsey noo? And what about Sir Jock?'

In fact, using discreet channels to the powers-that-be, Stein indicated that a knighthood should be awarded to the club's veteran chairman, who soon after became Sir Robert Kelly. Stein was given a CBE.

It was a result so great in its impact that it even briefly united both halves of the Old Firm. The paper claimed: 'Celtic and Rangers fans waltzed arm-in-arm along Argyle Street. One Rangers fan said: "It's a great night for Glasgow. There will be another great one next Wednesday when Rangers play Bayern Munich in Germany." Rangers boss Scot Symon praised Celtic: "What a wonderful victory. It was a tremendous display by a great Glasgow team who played their hearts out to the end. Mr Stein must be a very proud man tonight. I only hope we pull off the double next week."'

There was a crisis in the Middle East but Celtic took over Page One on the Saturday morning as well. The *Record* sent a reporter in a plane to witness the new European Champions' arrival back at Parkhead. 'It looked as if the whole city was pivoting round Celtic,' he said. Over 60,000 fans packed into Celtic Park, and 200,000 more lined the streets to cheer the team as they drove from Glasgow Airport.

'This has been a once-in-a-lifetime happening for me,' said Bob Kelly. 'The wonderful thing is that not just Celtic fans are cheering us. They've come from all over Scotland.'

'The new masters of Europe can become masters of world football,' claimed Hugh Taylor in his post-Lisbon summing-up.

The euphoria didn't go on for ever, but it was good while it lasted. Celtic's reign as Champions of Europe was short, losing to the Soviet side, Dynamo Kiev, in the first round of the 1967–68 competition. But much worse followed when they took part in the World Club Championship against the South American side, Racing Club of Argentina.

The first match of the two-legged affair was held in Glasgow, and a Billy McNeill goal gave Celtic a 1–0 lead, which Hugh Taylor described as 'halfway to the stars'. However, the Celtic players got their first taste of the tactics that were to cruelly scar the other games. Taylor said: 'Racing were hard men. Perhaps too hard at times. But that's how they play it down Argentine way.' There was a typical Scottish storm in a tea-cup, when Celtic wanted to play Jimmy Johnstone although he was suspended. They claimed the ban didn't apply to the World Club Championship, and the SFA said otherwise. Eventually Celtic won that little war.

The return leg in Buenos Aires started with a sensation, when Celtic keeper Ronnie Simpson was attacked on the field even before the kick-off and John Fallon had to take over in goal.

Tommy Gemmell scored from a penalty and Johnstone had a goal disallowed, but Racing scored twice for a 2–1 win. This was the kind of day which ages newspaper executives, and pushes them towards a place in the great press-box in the sky. Instead of too little happening, there was too much: a gunman ran amok at a school in Dundee and killed a teacher; Rangers sacked manager Scot Symon; and there was trouble in Buenos Aires.

The *Record*, as always, coped superbly and Taylor revealed that Celtic had made a sensational threat to pull out of the play-off in the Uruguayan capital of Montevideo unless they got better protection.

It's incredible now, when a vast media army follows the Scotland international team and the major clubs abroad, that for that trip to South America there were only six of us from Scotland – Taylor, John Mackenzie, James Sanderson, Alex Cameron, John Blair and myself.

The third game, in Montevideo, was a débâcle. Celtic had three players sent off, Johnstone, Bobby Lennox and John Hughes, and in the last minute Bertie Auld was also sent off by the Paraguayan referee, Dr Rodolfo Osario, but the Celtic player refused to leave the field. The referee also missed the incident that received the most attention in TV highlights shown after the match. Tommy Gemmell kicked a Racing player up the backside. The Argentinian team had two players dismissed in this 1967 version of the Battle of the River Plate and Taylor wrote:

'Celtic are bitterly ashamed *not* because they lost 1–0 to Racing, the most professional assassins the world has ever known, *not* because they seldom touched top form, but because they lost their heads and the great reputation they have built up over the years. There can be no excuses. Celtic came down to Racing's level and engaged in a running street brawl with their vicious opponents.

'Celtic chairman Bob Kelly summed it up bitterly, but fairly, when he told me today: "I never thought I would live to see the day when a Celtic team behaved in this fashion. I know there were reasons, but it was sad to see our boys reduced to Racing's level."'

Taylor, however, defended Celtic stoutly:

'If I had been playing for Celtic I'd have been punching and kicking and hacking with the toughest of them. These Celtic players are Scots. They have spirit and courage and great hearts. They can only take so much.

'They were wrong to retaliate. Wrong to throw discipline to the brisk South American breezes. But I cannot blame them. Yes, I'm bitter. This was not football. This was war. It was jungle savagery, calculated viciousness.'

The Celtic board fined their entire team £250 each, and Auld and Hughes were each fined £50 by the SFA for their part in the affair. Johnstone was severely censured and Lennox, who was the victim of mistaken identity, was exonerated. It was a black chapter for Celtic, and Scottish football.

Sadly, the dream double of twin European victories involving Celtic and Rangers didn't come true. Rangers had to wait until their 1972 European Cup-Winners' Cup victory in Barcelona against Moscow Dynamo made it third time lucky in the competition. They had lost to Italian team Fiorentina in the first-ever final of the tournament – at that time a two-legged affair. Even in 1961 Italian clubs snapped up the best in Europe, and Fiorentina's top star was a dapper little Swedish winger named Kurt Hamrin.

Six years later Rangers failed again, an even crueller blow

to the pride of the Ibrox club. Their opponents were the famed German side, Bayern Munich, with a new rising star in their line-up named Franz Beckenbauer. The venue was Nuremberg in Germany, and it took one goal in extra time to deprive Scot Symon – their first manager to take them into competitive matches in Europe and the first British boss to reach a European final – of the honour he had come so close to winning. No defeat in a final is ever the right time for any club, but this one was an especially sore blow for Ibrox to bear, coming only six days after Celtic's victory in Lisbon. The repercussions rumbled on and on. The next season Symon was sacked in one of the most shameful episodes in Rangers' long history.

But by season 1971–72 they had regrouped and, led by the redoubtable Willie Waddell, with Jock Wallace beside him as coach, they had won through to the final of the Cup-Winners' competition again, and defeated their old adversaries, Bayern Munich, in the semi-final. The venue this time was the fabulous Nou Camp stadium in Barcelona and Rangers' opponents were Moscow Dynamo – old adversaries from the end of the Second World War when the two clubs had fought out a memorable 2–2 draw.

Before the final, at the Scottish Football Writers Association Player of the Year dinner in Glasgow, the main speaker, former Prime Minister Harold Wilson, had joked: 'I feel sorry for the Spanish fans. Who do they support in the final? The all-Protestant Glasgow Rangers or the Godless Communists of Moscow Dynamo?' But not even a politician's foresight could have predicted what did happen as the wide-eyed Spaniards watched the Battle of Barcelona, which, sadly for Rangers, will always be linked with their greatest night in a European competition.

Rangers flew to Spain with one doubt in their team line-up: Andy Penman, Alfie Conn and Derek Parlane were vying for the one undecided place. The *Record* reported that Willie Waddell was astonishingly relaxed on the eve of the game, and when the team was announced Conn won his way into the side which consisted of McCloy, Jardine, Mathieson, Greig, Derek Johnstone, Smith, McLean, Conn, Stein, MacDonald and Willie Johnston. 'The men who can become immortal,' said the paper on the morning of the match, Wednesday, 24 May 1972.

And in words which sounded similar to the cinema newsreels of the time, the *Record* jauntily detailed the fans' exploits: 'The rain in Spain was like home from home for the Rangers supporters. But the damp weather didn't dampen their spirits. After all, they're not in Barcelona for a tanning. They're there to see Rangers take the European Cup-Winners' Cup against Moscow Dynamo. And the prospect of that is enough to bring out sunny smiles from anyone.'

Rangers romped to an incredible 3–0 lead in the final, two goals in the first half from Colin Stein and Willie Johnston added a third three minutes after half-time. But the Russians fought back with two goals, the second only three minutes from full-time, and it was a nail-biting finish as Rangers clung to their narrow lead.

It should have been Rangers' greatest night of glory in Europe for bearded skipper John Greig and his team-mates. It would have been, but on Thursday morning, 25 May 1972, the headline on Page One blazed out: 'THE SHAME IN SPAIN'.

Alex Cameron reported:

'Thousands of Rangers fans fought a pitched battle with baton-swinging Spanish police here last night. It happened at the end of the most unruly major European match ever.

'The scenes after Rangers had beaten Moscow Dynamo 3–2 in the Cup-Winners' Cup were fantastic. It was chaos. A total shambles. A blot on sport and those who watch it.

'It took the Rangers players nearly ten minutes to fight their way through the mobbing, milling thousands, who rushed on to the pitch in the worst mass invasion ever at a big game in Europe.

'It was the fifth time the fans had scurried madly on to the great Barcelona pitch from their seats on the steep tiers of concrete. Finally, the pistol-packing policemen, who had shown total apathy, lost their heads at the end of the match. They charged into the crowd with batons swinging madly. Fans were bludgeoned to the ground.

'White-suited ambulancemen rushed around to attend to fans with blood streaming from their faces. The police charged the unruly mob three times, foot-long batons swinging like windmills among the Scots. But the most astonishing scene of all was when hordes of yelling fans leapt from the terracing and chased the police

The after-match agony of John Greig: The Rangers skipper is mobbed by invading fans at the end of the European Cup-Winners' Cup final victory against Moscow Dynamo in Barcelona.

halfway across the pitch in disorder.'

Photographers Eric Craig and Bob Campbell produced graphic pictures to go with the words. The front page was illustrated with a dramatic shot of John Greig, his face contorted in agony, as he was mobbed by his own club's jubilant fans. Greig was even denied the memory of the cup presentation, and the skipper's right to hold the trophy aloft on the pitch. The cup and medal ceremony was held deep inside the vast Nou Camp Stadium.

Spanish TV authorities, fearing their government's power would be weakened by the sight of one of the most massive displays against the police since the Civil War nearly three decades earlier, ordered the transmission from the match to be switched off. Alex Cameron thundered:

'This was the night Scottish football went mad. Thousands of Rangers fans turned the club's greatest victory in Europe into a sordid, unruly riot. What should have been the pay-off for the fans who have arrived here in 60 chartered planes, buses, cars and on foot, was turned into a total shambles.

'It was a marvellous sight to see these ardent Rangers fans spread about this huge stadium and clearly so desperate for a victory. But it was a terrible thing when they decided to take hold of the European Cup-Winners' Cup final and tear it apart in their outright unruliness.

'Nobody in his right mind, Scots or otherwise, could condone what happened. At the finish several Rangers fans clustered round me shouting: "How can we say sorry to the Spaniards? We are ashamed. This is not what we wanted for Rangers."

'On the morning after we should all have been so proud of Rangers we will go home in abject shame. One of the most hurt and close to tears when he spoke to reporters half an hour after the game was manager Willie Waddell. Before the match he thought all his problems were over. No manager should ever have to go out on to the pitch and wrestle with his own supporters. That completed our night of shame.'

It was made worse because there had been so much to admire in the Rangers team's display during the game and Ken Gallacher stressed in his match report:

'It was a tragedy for the thousands of decent fans who stayed in the stand and on the terracing they could not see John Greig, that great Rangers captain, hold aloft the trophy that had eluded them for so long.

'In that first half Rangers were magnificent – every single one of them – and after half-time they fought desperately against a Russian team which played with as much courage as any side I can remember in Europe. In that spell, when Rangers were in so much trouble, the coolness of Derek Johnstone and Dave Smith and the brilliant goalkeeping of Peter McCloy have to be mentioned, just as earlier in the game the goalscorers, Colin Stein and Willie Johnston, were the heroes. But it was a tragedy that this night of trial should have been spoiled by the fans.

'For the game, though, there can be nothing but praise. Praise for the way the goals were scored and praise, too, for the way they refused to give in under that tremendous Russian fightback. They lived dangerously to win that trophy, and they have won it. At last the Ibrox trophy room will house the European Cup-Winners' Cup. And even the second-half worries cannot take away the glory which was earned indeed in the epic battles across Europe.'

The following night 20,000 fans turned up to welcome the triumphant Rangers team back to their home ground: 'This was an Ibrox night of nights, a time to stand up and cheer. And they did, 20,000 of them, like cheering had just been invented,' said the paper.

The spotlight now moved into the tricky area of soccer diplomacy, and Rangers were fortunate. Their board of directors at the time was largely ineffective but in that sphere Willie Waddell was every bit as powerful in command as when he was a player. Moscow Dynamo manager Constantin Beskov had claimed in Barcelona minutes after the match that they wanted a replay. UEFA ruled against that but kicked Rangers out of European competitions for two years, later reduced to one year after a powerful plea by Waddell.

And in the years since, Rangers have worked hard to improve the behaviour of their fans abroad. Under the direction of security officer Alistair Hood, they have one of the most efficient and effective systems in football – so that in their great European campaign of 1992–93 the spotlight rightly went on their players, and not on unruly fans.

There was a gap of 11 years before a third success in Europe brought the Cup-Winners' Cup back to Scotland, and Alex Ferguson showed he was a managerial force to be reckoned with as he led Aberdeen to triumph. Their victory against the mighty Real Madrid in the Swedish seaport of Gothenburg put them in the first rank of Scottish clubs in Europe, right up with Celtic and Rangers.

And there to see it was Jock Stein, the man who had paved the way, and then Scotland team manager. Indeed, there was much of Stein's common-sense approach in Ferguson's attitude to the game. The Pittodrie boss insisted: 'We are dealing with the present Real players, not the side which last won a European trophy 17 years ago.' He threw in a little gamesmanship when he told the *Record*: 'Spanish football is not totally convincing at the highest level.'

Fergie's managerial opponent was the legendary Alfredo Di Stefano and the Aberdeen boss said: 'We'll make mistakes. But as long as we get it right on the park that's what counts. What a challenge it is for my players to perform on such a platform. How many players have ever had the opportunity to participate in such a showpiece? The biggest problem for us will be maintaining concentration. I don't want my players

169

admiring the marvellous setting. I want them to come off the park and be told how well they played.'

There was another link with that glory night in Lisbon. One of the spectators who travelled to Gothenburg was Celtic manager Billy McNeill, who had been boss at Pittodrie before he moved to Parkhead.

There was an exodus of Aberdeen fans to Sweden, and the *Record* told its readers:

'The Red Army became the Red Navy as they cast off on the P&O ferry, *St Clair*, at Aberdeen harbour. The seaborne invasion was thirsty work. P&O kept the fans happy with huge beer containers and 25,000 cans were stowed away. A company spokesman said: "We hope the supply will last the 30-hour trip." The banner-festooned *St Clair*, with 500 fans aboard, sailed to the cheers of 1,000 on the quayside and the skirl of the pipes.'

The team were also given a send-off to remember, a 19-year-old singing telegram girl, Tricia, in Aberdeen strip, stockings and suspenders. It was a present from the players' wives, the idea of Claire Miller, wife of Dons skipper, Willie, and the *Record* said:

'It was a wives' ploy in retaliation to a joke over sleeping arrangements by manager Alex Ferguson. He had sent out a spoof itinerary to the wives which said they would be sleeping in dormitories instead of a five-star luxury hotel. Claire said: "All the wives thought it would be better to send a real live, pretty telegram rather than the usual good luck messages."'

It worked a treat for on Thursday, 12 May 1983, Scotland woke up to see a slab of big, fat type across Page One which read: 'SUPER SUB JOHN', beside a picture of Aberdeen player John Hewitt with the Cup-Winners' Cup on top of his head. The paper said:

Previous page: Captain Marvel! Aberdeen skipper Willie Miller leads his victorious Aberdeen team on a 1983 lap of honour after their European Cup Winners' Cup triumph against Real Madrid in Gothenburg.

'It's the crowning glory for the hero of Scotland. Aberdeen's John Hewitt uses his head to lift the European Cup-Winners' Cup – just as he used his head to put paid to the finest football skills of Real Madrid. With just eight minutes of the final remaining, young John headed home the vital winning goal. 15,000 fans erupted. And thousands more in Aberdeen and through-out Scotland went out with a delirious dance of joy.'

The Aberdeen heroes were Leighton, Rougvie, Miller,

McLeish, McMaster, Cooper, Strachan, Simpson, Black, McGhee and Weir, and their five subs were Kennedy, Gunn, Watson, Hewitt and Angus.

Ian Broadley reported from the rain-soaked Ullevi Stadium in Gothenburg on the Dons' 2–1 extra-time triumph:

'Supersub John Hewitt earned Aberdeen their own place in the soccer history books with the extra-time goal which got Aberdeen their first-ever European success.

'With just eight minutes to go, the youngster, who had taken over from Eric Black, finished off marvellous interplay between Mark McGhee and Peter Weir with a fine header. That goal destroyed their once legendary opponents, Real Madrid. No victory was ever more deserved. The Dons had to withstand the physical tackling from their Spanish opponents and weak refereeing before claiming the European Cup-Winners' Cup.

'As the final whistle blew, manager Alex Ferguson – whose tactical expertise has carried Aberdeen into a new era to strike a highly significant blow for Scottish football – burst onto the heavy pitch to hug each of his heroes.'

Eric Black had scored first for Aberdeen in the seventh minute, only for the Spaniards to draw level seven minutes later, after a mistake by the Dons' defence, when Juanito scored with a penalty.

Not even the torrential rain dampened the spirit of the fans. The paper reported:

A hug from the boss, as delighted Alex Ferguson almost crushes Eric Black and John Hewitt, the players who scored the goals against Real Madrid which won the European Cup-Winners' Cup.

Success story: Aberdeen players return to Scotland in triumph with the European Cup-Winners' Cup in 1983.

173

Another final, another trophy: Aberdeen players celebrate after their 2–0 win against Hamburg in the European Super Cup.

'Two towns were painted well and truly red last night. The splash of gloss was provided by ecstatic Aberdeen fans in Gothenburg, Sweden, and at home after their team's marvellous Cup victory. In Gothenburg they swarmed around expensive bars and clubs. And it was the same story in Aberdeen itself where many of the pubs had their own version of extra-time. Earlier the city almost looked like a ghost town as stay-at-home fans huddled round TVs and radios. But seconds after that sweet final whistle the streets filled with overjoyed Aberdonians.'

Jock Stein hailed the victory: 'It's a marvellous night for our football and Aberdeen. They wobbled a bit after Real equalised, but from the beginning of the second half the Dons were on top and the Spaniards never really threatened. It was a tremendous victory and does Aberdeen and their fans great credit.'

Chairman Dick Donald agreed: 'Yes, it's certainly our finest moment. Now we've really made our name in Europe.'

'Everything was against a classic match. For all but the last 15 minutes of extra time the rain teemed down in torrents, drenching players and fans, but not dampening their wonderful enthusiasm,' wrote Alex Cameron.

Regular right-back Stuart Kennedy was out injured and Cameron said, 'Before the match the big doubt was about the full-back partnership of Doug Rougvie and John McMaster – but they were outstanding.' He saluted Ferguson: 'He has given Aberdeen new stature and won a place in football history alongside Jock Stein and Willie Waddell.' Perceptively, he added: 'Aberdeen will now face a fight to keep him at Pittodrie. Skipper Willie Miller and the other heroes of the Ullevi Stadium will hope the Dons board can persuade him to stay.'

He returned to the theme the next day in an interview with Ferguson, who admitted he was aware of talk that he would move from Pittodrie. 'It would take one helluva job to move me now. Five years can be a long time for a manager. If I were to receive an offer I would have to consider my family very carefully. My wife has made sacrifices in the past and I wonder if I could ask her to do it again. There are a lot of good reasons for remaining where I am.'

A leading Swedish paper claimed: 'A new team is born in Europe,' and meanwhile the players of that club were parading through Aberdeen in an open-topped bus. There was nothing unlucky about Page One for Friday the 13th, taken up almost completely with a smiling Alex Ferguson hugging goalscorers Eric Black and John Hewitt. None of them knew that three years ahead that 'helluva job' would come up for Ferguson when he moved to Manchester United to start his own history-making exploits at the world-famous Old Trafford club. There, he also met up with an old friend, the European Cup-Winners' Cup, but this time the red victory ribbons that draped the trophy in 1991 were the scarlet of United and not Aberdeen.

Before that, Ferguson guided the Dons to victory in the European Super Cup final. Taking part in the two-legged affair was one of the spin-offs for the victory in Gothenburg. They met European Cup-holders Hamburg, and it was game, set and match to Aberdeen. They played a no-scoring draw in Germany, and then romped to a 2–0 win at Pittodrie with goals by Neil Simpson and Mark McGhee.

The three European triumphs of Celtic, Rangers and Aberdeen stand out like beacons, for over the years Scotland's progress in Europe can best be described as patchy. Apart from Rangers' two unsuccessful attempts in the Cup-Winners' Cup final, though, there have been other near things. Celtic reached the final of the European Cup in 1970, only three years after Lisbon, but lost to Dutch side Feyenoord.

Then in 1987 Jim McLean came so close to taking Dundee United to a fourth win for Scotland. They lost 2–1 on aggregate in the final of the UEFA Cup to Swedish opponents Gothenburg. But they had the warm memory of a wonder win in their campaign against the multi-million-pound side of Barcelona. And UEFA also awarded the Tannadice club the Fair Play trophy for the good behaviour of the United fans in the two-legged final.

Rangers in season 1992–93 reached the Champions League stage of the European Cup, and came so close to making the final. Sadly, though, most of Scotland's sides have seen their hopes die in the early rounds of European competition. There would be no greater boost to the domestic game than for one of the leading teams to equal the achievements of those three giants, Celtic in '67, Rangers in '72 and Aberdeen in '83.

We live in hope!

Strike for Gold

Athletics Champions

The ultimate prize in sport is an Olympic gold medal. There have been massive changes since the modern Olympic Games started in 1896, but those shiny pieces of metal retain an eternal value. Scotland has won only two of those precious medals in track events –Eric Liddell in 1924 and Allan Wells in 1980.

If ever anyone lived up to the Corinthian ideals it was Liddell, whose story was told in the Oscar-winning film *Chariots of Fire*. He had rejected the chance of winning a gold medal in the 100 metres at the Paris Olympics because the heats took place on a Sunday and, as a committed Christian, he refused to run on the Sabbath.

Britain did win the sprint gold, when Harold Abrahams captured the event. But Liddell was not deprived of a medal either. He raced to spectacular victory in the 400 metres and the *Record* hailed the win on Page One of 12 July 1924.

The paper boasted under its masthead: 'The All-Scotland newspaper. Sale three times that of any other morning paper.' And for one penny the readers were told of Liddell's triumph. The main headline was 'SCOTS RUNNER'S FEAT', and with three decks of subheadings that read 'E.H. Liddell's triumph at Olympic Games', 'Wins 400 metres race' and 'Creates new world's record after thrilling finish'. There was a picture of him captioned 'Scotch Express' and the report was split into two parts, a description of the race and a biography of the winner. The first section, dated Paris, Friday, began:

'The Union Jack flew in proud majesty over the Colombes Stadium today, for the only final down for decision, the 400 metres flat, resulted in a great victory for Britain. The brilliant running of E.H. Liddell, the Edinburgh University student, was responsible and in covering the distance in 47.35 secs he created the third world's record in two days for this event. Guy Butler, the old Light Blue, was third, being separated from the winner by Fitch, the American, who, in the semi-final, returned 47.45 secs, beating Imbach's 48 seconds dead of yesterday.

'The race was the one bright spot in the afternoon's sport, for with the decathlon events occupying most of the programme the crowd had sunk more or less into apathy. It looked like being a dull afternoon. Suddenly the pipers of the Cameron Highlanders, who had assembled in the middle of the stadium, began playing and the crowd broke into cheers at the lively strains of a Scotch air.'

The report detailed the semi-finals and then went on: 'The final was even more thrilling. There was a gasp of astonishment when Eric Liddell, one of the most popular atheletes at Colombes, was seen to be a clear three yards ahead of the field at the half distance. Nearing the tape, Fitch and Butler strained every nerve and muscle to overtake him, but could make absolutely no impression on the inspired Scot. With 20 yards to go Fitch seemed to gain a fraction, but Liddell appeared to sense the American. And with head thrown back and chin thrust out in his usual style, he flashed past the tape to gain what was probably the greatest victory of the meeting.

'So far, certainly, there has not been a more popular win. The crowd went into a frenzy of enthusiasm, which was renewed when the loudspeaker announced that once again the world's record had gone by the board. The day really closed on this glorious note.'

The potted biography noted that Liddell was born in China on 16 January 1902. His father was a missionary in the Far East. It went on:

'He has held the 100 yards and 220 yards Scottish amateur

championships since 1921, and last month at Hampden in the SAAA Championship meeting he completed the triple event by adding to his list of triumphs the 440 yards race.

'Two years ago Liddell gave the English athletes a taste of his ability by romping home in the 100 yards and 220 yards at the British Championship gathering, and this year he won the 440 yards. If there have been ups and downs in his running career it's due to the fact that he is a student first and an athlete afterwards.'

Curiously, there was no mention that he had won caps for Scotland as a rugby international, or of his decision of conscience not to run in the 100 metres – for that was the stuff of a sporting legend.

But in April 1982, when *Chariots of Fire* was released, his sister, Jenny Sommerville, then 78, talked to the *Record* in her Edinburgh flat about her brother. 'Eric did what was perfectly normal to his way of life. Sunday was set aside for God. That was the code he lived by until his death.'

Under the heading 'A GLORIOUS VICTORY', an editorial purred:

'Eric Liddell's performance in the Olympic Games yesterday really merits the rather overworked adjective "sensational". His performance and that of Abrahams at the beginning of the week show that Great Britain can still produce athletes of the first rank. Our national aggregate of points in the Olympiad, however, suggests that we do not produce enough of them. Other countries, as we have pointed out before, are now taking their athletics more seriously than we do. The British team, as such, may quite conceivably move further and further down the points list in successive Olympiads, but doubtless there will always be one or two members who can give the world a thrill, and keep alive in us the good old British spirit of self-satisfaction.'

Not for the first time in compiling this book I'm struck by how often the same themes recur. The language of that 1924 editorial may be slightly stilted, but the message applies seven decades later.

Liddell, by then the Revd Eric, died – after 16 years of missionary work – in a Japanese internment camp in China, the land of his birth and his adoption, in February 1945, just a few months before the end of the Second World War.

*Heading for glory . . .
Margo and Allan Wells
preparing for Olympic
glory.*

A packed memorial service was held in Dundas Street Congregational Church, Glasgow. The scripture lesson was read by former Rangers player Alan Morton, and there were tributes from athlete Dunky Wright, former Scotland rugby captain John Bannerman, and Rangers manager Bill Struth. Liddell had often run at Ibrox in the famous Rangers Sports, the curtain-raiser to the football season, and it was Struth who, in a phrase that shines like a beacon through the years, told the congregation: 'Sport gave to Eric Liddell its highest honours; nevertheless, it is true to say that he honoured sport rather than sport honouring him.'

The link with Liddell was maintained when, in July 1980, the next Scot to win an Olympic gold medal, Allan Wells, roared his way to the 100 metres title in Moscow. After the race he told Alex Cameron: 'I'm flattered to be following the great Eric Liddell as a gold winner on the track after 56 years. I know Harold Abrahams won gold in the sprint at that same Olympic Games in Paris. But I know all about Liddell's principles, which forced him to miss the 100 metres because it was run on a Sunday.'

No one had ever heard of boycotts in Liddell's time, but by the time Allan Wells was competing the Olympics were rocked by countries pulling out for political reasons. The 1980 event was threatened because the world was aghast when the host nation, the Soviet Union, invaded Afghanistan. America's

President Jimmy Carter refused to let his nation compete, and Prime Minister Margaret Thatcher made it clear she didn't want any British participation either. But the Brits went ahead and the *Record* told the story of Wells' anguish at the end of the race in Moscow. Accompanied by a picture of him with the precious medal, the paper said:

'This is the moment that at one time never looked like happening – Scotland's Alan Wells proudly wearing the coveted 100 metres Olympic Gold Medal. The medal was won by a hair's breadth from Cuban Silvio Leonard with Petar Petrov of Bulgaria trailing third. But Allan's golden glory came only after an agony of waiting. Ten nerve-wracking minutes before the judges decided he had taken first place with a nod and a push of the chest to cross the line just ahead of Leonard.

'There was a hold-up of two and a quarter hours before the Edinburgh sprinter was able to pass the drugs test. Then the tension ended and 28-year-old Allan climbed the podium in the Moscow Stadium to receive the gold. The race produced one of the most dramatic finishes of the Games. Not even the sophisticated electronic timing equipment could split the Scot and the Cuban, each of whom had a time of 10.25 seconds. When Allan saw the action replay on the stadium's huge TV screens he was certain he had won, throwing his arms in the air and doing a lap of honour.

'But for millions watching TV – and Allan's wife, Margot – there were nagging doubts. As the two sprinters crossed the line, 27-year-old Margot cupped her head in her hands, crying, "He's lost, he's lost." Tears were streaming down her cheeks and when the final verdict came, she said: "When he came to the line, I screamed, 'Dip, Allan, dip!' Thank God we've done it."'

Wells told his story exclusively to Alex Cameron:
'When I stood on the winner's podium my one regret was that the national anthem, and not 'Flower of Scotland', was ringing round the ground. There can be no better moment in a man's life, and the truth is I felt very Scottish. I would have liked this to be obvious on such a memorable occasion for me.

'Because it wasn't my fastest time people are already asking if I was pleased with the way I ran. Pleased? I've got the gold medal, haven't I? Now I have the title of fastest man on earth. It still seems a bit incredible. I think we should now take a sword and cut the gold in two. My win was a team effort and Margot, my wife, was the other part of the team.'

It was a wonderful achievement for the 27-year-old former long-jumper who once had a secret ambition to play for Hearts. Wells, the son of a blacksmith, had twice turned down scholarships to American universities because he and his wife couldn't bear to be parted from their cat, Gaby. He even came so close to making it a double gold strike. He took a silver in the 200 metres, finishing one 200th of a second behind Italy's Pietro Mienna.

It seemed that day that Olympic fame would eventually beckon for 16-year-old Linsey Macdonald from Dunfermline. She took part in the 400 metres final, and although she finished last, she was the youngest-ever Olympic track finalist. Sadly, her promise never flowered into future Olympic successes.

Four years after Moscow the joy turned to anguish for defending champion Wells when he finished last in the semi-finals. 1984 was the year of American superman Carl Lewis, who went on to win the 100 metres crown. Alex Cameron described it as 'a race into athletic oblivion'. Wells said:

'I haven't slept all night worrying about the reaction of the people who have supported me so well. Maybe I shouldn't have competed at all and avoided this situation. Right now, I feel nothing.

'I simply wasn't conditioned right for so big a race. I don't know what happened. Today I have a foot injury and I must simply believe that this was the reason. I don't want to make excuses. I had nothing to give when I wanted to go into top gear at 60 metres.

'It didn't bother me having Carl Lewis on my immediate right in lane six. And I don't agree his speed broke my morale. It was all so out of character, so unusual. I can't say how terrible I feel after this worst moment of my life.'

Wells eventually retired with the memories of a string of Commonwealth victories, plus other major wins – but nothing could top that win in Moscow.

The trio of athletes who succeeded him to the rare position of being household names in Scotland were Tom McKean,

Back in the big-time: Liz McColgan celebrating a 3000 metres indoor win in the British-USA contest at the Kelvin Hall, Glasgow, just weeks after giving birth to her daughter in 1991.

Liz McColgan and Yvonne Murray.

McColgan, born in Dundee in May 1964, won silver in the Olympic 10,000 metres in Seoul in 1988 and has twice won Commonwealth titles at the same distance. She's also won marathons in places as far apart as New York and Tokyo, and held the world's half-marathon title. Her greatest achievement, however, was winning the World Championship 10,000 metres crown in Japan in 1991. And on 31 August she filled the *Record*'s front page, plus pages 2, 12, 13 and the back page. That amount of space is only given to someone very special.

Page One showed the golden wonder draped in a Union Jack, but she had a grim message despite her glory. 'I MAY HAVE TO QUIT SCOTLAND' was the headline. Inside, Alex Cameron reported:

'Superstar Liz McColgan dropped a bombshell after striking gold yesterday. Liz became the darling of all Britain by winning our only World Championships gold medal. But then she warned, "I may have to quit Scotland." If she doesn't get sponsor support, Liz reckons she will have to leave Scotland and run for big money in the US. "If I have to, and it would be a last resort, I'll move to America," she said.'

In a separate story, Cameron went on:

'Liz McColgan, Queen of Scottish athletics, yesterday became Britain's number-one track star. Her shattering 25-lap gold run here in Tokyo was the greatest distance ever run by a Briton – male or female. Supermum Liz raced to the World Championship 10,000 metres title in 31 minutes 14.31 seconds.

'Liz became the first British woman to win world track gold since Ann Packer at the Tokyo Olympics in 1964. Britain's coach Frank Dick described it as "a destruction – the most impressive demonstration of power and endurance I've ever witnessed".

'She declared: "I won my gold for Scotland and I got it the hard way, leading from the start. My husband Peter told me I could run away from anyone, and he was right. Going out fast to get a good position was important." At one stage Ethiopian Derartu Tulu went past her, with 8½ laps to go. Liz went on: "She tried to slow it, instead of trying to go away. So I went into the lead again. She was running really close to me and kept tripping me. At one point I went off the track and I thought, God, I'll be disqualified. She wanted to hang on for a sprint finish but I thought, Stuff it, you've worked too hard to lose like that. So I went on and she dropped really quickly after a couple more laps.

'"If you want it you've got to go for it, so I just kept saying to myself 'work, work, work'. I proved I wanted it more than anybody else. From 600 metres out I knew I had won. I just relaxed and enjoyed the feeling of winning. I never run badly at a major championships. I'm tough. I don't pull the wool over my eyes. I'm not really worried about breaking world records. I have nothing to prove."

'Just in case anyone missed the point, the intensely competitive McColgan rammed it home: "It's the championships that matter and once I have the Olympic title in Barcelona, then I'll think about world-best times. I've proved again I'm Scotland's number one. I'm the World Champion."'

By December TV viewers in an all-Britain poll voted her BBC Sports Personality of the Year, and there was an appearance on *This is Your Life*. But there was no glory gold for Liz in the Olympics in Barcelona. She could only finish fifth and she told the *Record*: 'I ran a bad race and I don't understand it.'

Alex Cameron wrote the day after: 'Yesterday she was up before the lark on her way home to see daughter Eilish whom she badly missed during her month-long separation. Had she moved as fast in the race the gold would have been hers. McColgan will not give up, nor should she. She is a thoroughly honest and clean competitor in the suspect world of athletics.'

Britain's director of coaching, Frank Dick, was quoted in the paper: 'Liz showed her courage the way she went out front. She was the one with the bottle. Obviously her legs gave in but the people at home shouldn't think badly of her. She did her best and gave everything. It wasn't good enough on the night, but that's what the Olympics are all about.'

Yvonne Murray was born the same year as Liz McColgan, 1964, and she won a bronze in the 3,000 metres at the Seoul Olympics in 1988. The *Record* honoured Yvonne and Liz McColgan, who had won Silver in the gruelling 10,000 metres. *Record* Editor-in-Chief Endell Laird emphasised the pride the paper took in the women's thrilling performances. 'It

was wonderful to see two Scots doing so well at the pinnacle of sport. My strong feeling was that we should recognise such an outstanding Scottish double.'

The women were presented with specially struck medals, crafted in nine-carat gold and worth more than £1,000 each. At the presentation luncheon Liz revealed both she and Yvonne were avid readers of the *Record*, especially the crossword. 'It helps us to relax without having to bash our brains in.'

The major highpoint of Yvonne's career was in 1990 when she shared a double Scottish triumph at the European Championships in Split, Yugoslavia. The paper told the proud story:

'Millions of TV fans all over Europe saluted the pride of Scotland last night. Tom McKean brushed aside his loser's label once and for all with a wonderful run to grab the European 800 metres crown. Yvonne Murray wept tears of joy after a true-grit gold-medal run in the 3,000 metres.

'The super Scots, both coached by Tommy Boyle, hugged in celebration after Murray's triumph. Mac the Flop became Mac the Magnificent as he more than made up for his spectacular failures at the '87 World Championships, the '88 Olympics and this year's Commonwealth Games. Cruelly tagged as having no stomach for the big occasion he proved the critics wrong with a flaw-

Opposite: The loneliness of the long-distance runner: Yvonne Murray in action.

Liz McColgan with baby Eilish, in 1991.

less display of courage.

'For McKean it was the end of a personal nightmare. The 26-year-old Bellshill battler ran the perfect two-lap race. He burst into the lead at the break and defied anyone to get past him. Doing it the hard way he held off all-comers after a brisk first lap of 51.31 seconds and then hit the accelerator on the home straight to win by some five metres in a superb 1 minute 44.76 seconds. "I proved I can do it," he said.

'Tearful Yvonne from Musselburgh won in similar style to McKean. She made a break just under 600 metres from the finish and bravely held off Russian danger girl Yelena Romanova. "Tommy said to me before the race, the person who wins is going to be the person who wants it most – and I wanted it most," she gasped. Murray, who becomes the first Scottish woman ever to win a European gold and one of only a handful of British girls to do so, had actually to be calmed by Boyle on the warm-up track, so excited was she by McKean's victory. Afterwards, she could not wait to stand on the gold-medal podium, saying: "I've always wanted to see what it was like to see the British flag going up first." Murray's winning time was 8 mins 43.06 secs.'

McKean is a constant puzzle to athletics fans. He failed twice in the Olympics, and at other major championships, but

Award time for coach Tommy Boyle (left) and his two star athletes, Tom McKean and Yvonne Murray.

he also made good in different competitions. Less than a year after his flop in Barcelona he was on top of the world again. This time, the *Record* reported from Toronto, Canada, on another night of shared glory for Tommy Boyle's 'twins'.

'Super Scots Yvonne Murray and Tom McKean were in dreamland last night after striking double gold in the World Indoor Championships. It was a fitting finale to follow little-known Glaswegian David Strang's silver streak in the 1,500 metres the night before. It was all the more praiseworthy as the tartan double act roared home in the 3,000 then 800 metres to give Britain its only golden celebrations.

'Murray struck the first blow for Britain and was again on top of the world – just months after she had been on the verge of quitting the sport in despair. And as she celebrated she dedicated her victory to the coach who helped talk her out of retirement after the Barcelona trauma. "This is for Tommy Boyle," said the rejuvenated 28-year-old. "I'd been through a bad patch, but he sent me a book of poetry which included the words 'Never give up on your dreams'. I'd come close to quitting after the Olympics but he told me not to throw in the towel. There were a lot of traumatic phone-calls between the two of us and I had to do a lot of soul-searching."'

There was a special reason for Scotland to cheer at the 1986 European Championships in Stuttgart, when Ayr's Brian Whittle ran the third leg of the 4 × 400 metres relay minus one shoe. It made him a TV star, for he produced the race of his life to help the British to a gold medal.

Scotland traditionally took a string of major honours at the Empire Games, later Commonwealth Games. There were none better than the 1970 Commonwealth Games in Edinburgh, which did really live up to the tag of 'The Friendly Games'.

Record boxing writer Dick Currie, meeting the Duke of Edinburgh, reminded him the last time they talked was 16 years earlier, when the Duke had presented Dick with a boxing gold medal at the Vancouver Games.

Glasgow's Lachie Stewart beat Australian world record-holder Ron Clarke into second place in the 10,000 metres. The Scot won the gold on a breakfast of cornflakes, four biscuits and a cup of tea.

Tom McKean (left) and Brian Whittle.

The crowd sang 'Will ye no come back again' to the Queen at the end of the Games and on Monday, 27 July 1970, the *Record* said:

'Scotland paid a golden farewell to the Commonwealth Games in Edinburgh on Saturday with a fairytale ending that will never be forgotten. The dream finale after more than a week of the greatest athletics spectacle ever staged in Britain came in the 5,000 metres, the event that was billed as "The Race of the Century".

'Scotland's runners rose magnificently to the occasion when Ian Stewart and Ian McCafferty left the great Kip Keino in third place with other world stars, including Ron Clarke, trailing behind. Half a million spectators turned up at Meadowbank Stadium. Now the curtain has come down and Meadowbank is empty. But not for long. Scotland's stadium is recognised as *the* place in Britain, perhaps in all Europe, to stage meetings.'

But it all went wrong 16 years later when the Games returned to Edinburgh. The African and Caribbean nations boycotted the Games because they objected to a New Zealand rugby tour of South Africa and to Mrs Thatcher's attitude to economic sanctions against the apartheid-ridden Republic. The organising committee almost went bankrupt. They were saved by the crashing intervention of Mirror Group Newspapers publisher, Robert Maxwell. Will ye no come back again? The answer from everyone connected with those bleak, rain-swept Games was 'We wish we hadn't'.

But the Commonwealth Games also provide many wonderful moments, none more so than the most recent Games, the 1994 gathering at Victoria, British Columbia, when late-night TV viewers in Britain, watching the events in Canada, cheered on Yvonne Murray to victory in the gruelling 10,000 metres. That was a night to remember for Yvonne and delighted Scots everywhere!

Opposite: Carrying a torch: Yvonne Murray launches an appeal for the British Olympic Fund in 1991.

191

The Game We Gave the World

A Century of Great Golfers

Golf is the universal Scottish sport, whether it is played in the snooty surroundings of the Honourable Company of Edinburgh Golfers at Muirfield or at one of the many packed municipal courses. In fact, as the famous golf commentator Henry Longhurst once remarked in the inter-war years, no one would give a second glance to someone walking down Glasgow's Sauchiehall Street with a bag of golf clubs over their shoulder, but every head would turn in Regent Street, London.

Yet in the country that rightly regards itself as the home of golf, and can trace its history back to 1457, the number of Scottish golfers this century who have won the number-one prize, the Open Championship, remain pitifully few. They include Sandy Herd, James Braid, George Duncan, Jock Hutchison, Tommy Armour and Sandy Lyle – all apart from Lyle in the first third of the century.

Herd, born in St Andrews, changed golf for ever when he won the title at Hoylake in 1902 with a revolutionary ball imported from America which had a rubber core. The Haskell ball, as it was known, was eight times more expensive than a

Opposite: Dress styles may have changed, but a perfect golf swing remains the same, as Tommy Armour – the Open winner of 1931 – shows.

193

normal ball, and Herd used the same one for four rounds.

Braid, born in Fife in 1870, was a member of the 'Great Triumvirate', along with Harry Vardon and John Taylor, who ruled golf before the First World War. He won the Open five times between 1901 and 1910, and his record 291 at Prestwick in 1908 stood until Bobby Jones beat it at St Andrews in 1927.

Look back to the *Record* of Saturday, 20 June 1908, which told of Braid's win at the height of Britain's Edwardian summer. The paper of that day also reported that the British Fleet, 54 warships, were on a visit to Norway; 250,000 Suffragettes were holding a votes-for-women rally in London's Hyde Park; and a day-trip on the paddle-steamer *Columba* from the Broomielaw to Ardrishaig – with breakfast, lunch and tea on board – cost 10s 6d. It was a very different-looking *Daily Record* – even bigger than the size of today's broadsheets, such as *The Independent* – and it had no pictures, only line drawings, and even they were few and far between.

The headlines read 'EPOCH-MAKING GOLF AT PRESTWICK', followed by 'Braid wins championship and creates a record', plus 'Nine strokes better than Harry Vardon's best'. And, in the small type used at the time, the anonymous reporter wrote:

'What has been an extraordinary week's golf culminated in the establishment of performances never before heard of in the history of the Open Championship; and the event of 1908 is certain to go down in the annals of the game as one abnormal in many phases.

'The indications given yesterday in these columns that James Braid would enrol himself alongside Harry Vardon and Tom Morris, jun, as winner of the blue ribbon for the fourth occasion, and that the record score of 296, to the credit of Jack White, over the four rounds constituting the event, would be broken, were fully realised. In these circumstances alone there is ample scope for earmarking the latest championship as the greatest event that has ever taken place in the realm of golf.

'Favoured by delightful conditions, suitable alike for the golfer and spectator, Prestwick was liberally inundated with arrivals by train from every direction; and at least 7,000 or 8,000 must have been assembled on the historic links – the biggest crowd seen in the West of Scotland, the international foursomes at Troon three years ago excepted.'

Braid took up most of the report and the Walton Heath professional's golf (he held the post for 45 years) was described:

'Followed by thousands, he gave a most brilliant display, driving powerfully and undeviatingly straight, while his iron play was no less effective. His putting was again capital, the worst being the eighth green, where he took three to hole out. A magnificent physique helped him considerably.

'Braid's winning score of 291 is nine better than Harry Vardon's winning score five years ago: and all the talk of 300 not being broken has been belied. The question no doubt will be raised whether James Braid is not the finest golfer of all time. One thing at any rate is to be said – he is the headiest. His extrication from serious difficulties near the finish of his final round at St Andrews three years ago, his remarkable finish at Muirfield a year later and the wonderful preservation of temper yesterday at a crucial stage stamp him as a golfer of unique temperamental endowment.'

His four rounds were 70, 72, 77, 72. Beside the report R.W. Forsyth in Glasgow advertised golf bags at 4s 9d and 7s 6d.

George Duncan, born in Methlick, Aberdeenshire, won the first Open Championship after the First World War, held in 1920 at Deal. He was followed by Jock Hutchison, winner the following year at St Andrews, his native town. But by that time Hutchison was an American-based Scot, and he was the first of many to take the famous old claret jug overseas after he beat amateur Roger Wethered in a 36-hole play-off.

Ten years later, in 1931, another Scots-American, Tommy Armour, was the winner at Carnoustie. After that there was a long, long wait until 1985 when Sandy Lyle, Midlands-born of Scottish parents, won at Sandwich.

Edinburgh-born Armour had gone to America with the Great Britain amateur Walker Cup team in 1922 and stayed on. His achievement at Carnoustie, the first Open to be held there, was even more meritorious because he had lost an eye in the First World War. The *Record* pulled out all the stops for this victory. Page One proudly proclaimed on 6 June 1931: 'How I won the Open Championship – Tommy Armour's own story'.

There was a picture of the winner, flanked by drawings of two flags, the Star-Spangled Banner and the Lion Rampant.

Armour's account dwarfed the early signs of the forthcoming financial crisis which toppled the Labour Government of the time, and the news that London pilot C.W.A. Scott had set a new record by flying from Australia to England in under 11 days.

It was the final round of 71 which won the title for Armour ahead of Argentinian Jose Jurado who could only finish with a 77 for an aggregate 297, one behind the victor. Armour wrote:

'I had a lot of luck and when I holed out my last putt I had no hope of triumph. I played two rounds today that I never want to go back on; my golf when I equalled the record of the course was as good as I could do in the wind, but although my aggregate was, to a figure, the one I predicted would win the Cup, it seemed to me that Jose Jurado held so great a lead he must eclipse my lead.

'I concluded my round more than an hour before Jurado and by that mysterious way that news travels across the links I learned that the gallant South American had dropped a stroke of his lead on my ninth-hole figures and that disaster at the fourteenth saw the end of the lead of five strokes with which he started out.

'Then came the wringing moments of waiting and I shall not describe my emotions as I watched Jurado's putt of four yards on the home green. The little white sphere rolled swiftly at the hole. No one moved. The ball seemed dead at the disc. Its pace slackened. It rolled feebly. I was champion golfer. My ambition was fulfilled.'

Jurado had needed a four to tie, and among the most disappointed spectators was one of his biggest fans, the Prince of Wales, who was later King Edward VIII and Duke of Windsor. The Prince was a keen golfer and the paper reported:

'It was Jurado's round to which the Prince confined his attention. He appeared on the course about 11 o'clock, watched Henry Cotton drive from the 16th tee, then cut across country to the "South American" hole to see the man he first met in South America, and who taught something more about the game the Prince loves so much.

'Many of the spectators were more anxious to see the Prince than the golfers and the golf. Consequently, as

HRH walked from the tee to the green, he was invariably followed by a crowd consisting generally of girls who seemed unwilling to drag themselves away from his vicinity.

'It was clear from some of his remarks and gestures that he was hoping for the best from his friend Jurado. When the best did not show up His Royal Highness showed his disappointment.

'The great crowd could hardly believe its eyes when it saw Jurado's tee shot at the 17th flop into the burn and his second with a brassie catch a bunker. Four to the green and two putts gave Jurado a 6. Then he needed a 4 to tie with Armour.

'The ball rolled towards the hole but stayed out no more than two inches to the left. Jurado smiled a little wanly and tapped the ball into the cup for a 5. The crowd applauded a great effort which had just failed.'

At the presentation ceremony Armour emphasised his Scottish roots. Said the report: 'As he received the Cup from the Earl of Airlie, Armour talked of Scotland as "my own country", and added: "I shall be a Scotsman all my life. At least, I hope so."' And in his own account of his victory he told the *Record*:

'I am taking the Cup back for another trip across the Atlantic, but I am a Scotsman and learned my golf on the Braid Hills of Edinburgh. I had an advantage over the contenders from abroad for I must have played from my boyhood for twenty summers at Carnoustie. I played hundreds of rounds here in my amateur days and, moreover, the air suits me, although I did feel the cold.'

Fast forward now to Monday, 22 July 1985. Alister Nicol began his Open Championship report:

'Alexander Walter Barr Lyle, as Scottish as they come in spite of his soft Midlands accent, is Britain's first Open Champion since Tony Jacklin and Scotland's first for 54 years. And Sandy won the world's oldest championship by producing gutsy, fighting golf when it was most needed at tough Royal St George's.

'Two behind Australian tough guy David Graham with six holes to play, the 27-year-old Scot then uncorked successive birdies at the 14th and 15th which knocked the stuffing out of the rest of the field for a final round 70 and

Sandy Lyle takes an iron to blast the ball off the tee.

two-over-par 282 total.

'Sandy has so much natural ability it was almost inevitable that one day he would take golf's most glittering prize. He has often been accused of not trying. But inside that placid exterior Sandy churns up as much as the next man. He also has that wonderful ability to shrug off what many people regard as disasters.'

That was shown at his last hole when he made a bogey five, and settled down to watch Bernhard Langer and David Graham, both of whom could have caught him. Nicol said: 'Langer actually had a chip to force the first-ever five-hole play-off in Open history – and it almost went in. But as he watched it run over the hole Sandy Lyle knew that he had finally made golfing history himself – and made millions of Scots the happiest golfers in the world.'

The *Record* was at Augusta for the Masters three years later and under the back-page headline 'A STROKE OF GENIUS', Alister Nicol wrote:

'Sandy Lyle was last night crowned king of golf in dramatic fashion. The super Scot holed an eight-foot birdie putt on Augusta's 18th green to go into the history books as the first British winner of the coveted US Masters.

'And as he savoured his moment of magic, he admit-

Greens for go! Star Scots Sam Torrance (above) and Sandy Lyle competing in the Bells Scottish Open at Gleneagles in 1993.

199

ted, "I thought it was all over when I drove into a bunker at the 18th. Then I hit one of the best shots of my career with a 7-iron. I can't tell you how great it is to be the first Scot to win the Masters. Even though I have lived all my life in England, my mother and father are from Glasgow. I have nothing but Scottish blood in my veins, and I am proud of it."

'Now, undoubtedly the world's number one – just as his dad had been predicting he would be for years – there was a bonus for Lyle. His father Alex was there to see it all.'

Lyle, after a series of disappointments, is still striving to reach again those twin peaks in his career, but what wonderful reading they make looking back on it today.

Sam Torrance has battled to win a major title, and is still trying. But if the very top prizes have eluded him he's got plenty of consolation – more than £2 million after two decades as a top-class golfer. And he, too, played himself into golfing history. The *Record*'s front page on Monday, 16 September 1985, told it all with a headline: 'SPRAY IT AGAIN SAM!' and a picture of Seve Ballesteros drenching Torrance with champagne. The story explained:

'It rained champagne last night for Super Scot Sam Torrance, the man who won golf's Ryder Cup for Europe for the first time in 28 years. One hole down with two to play, the husky Scottish champion from Largs needed to win to beat the might of America. And he did – with two magnificent birdies.

'Even Concorde did a victory roll to celebrate Europe's 16½–11½ whipping of the might of American golf in the Bell's Ryder Cup at The Belfry last night. But not even the roar of the supersonic jet's powerful engines could drown the yells of jubilation from the 30,000 fans who saw the Yanks lose for the first time since 1957. And spearheading the historic win for Tony Jacklin's European heroes were the great Scots, Sandy Lyle and Sam Torrance.'

Nicol described how Europe needed only one point for an historic victory:

'Enter Sam Torrance. The Scottish champion, who had been struggling with his game all week, found himself three down with eight to play against lanky US Open

Champion, Andy North. It seemed to all the golfing world like a lost cause. But suddenly he found his rhythm. Torrance won the 11th in par to reduce the deficit to two, and when North lost the long 15th with a bogey Torrance then set about cutting him down to size with a vengeance.

'He missed a good chance on the 16th and it was then that Jacklin told him exactly what was required: "If you win this match you will win the Ryder Cup."'

'An indifferent drive saw him select a 3-wood for his second shot to the 17th, with Ballesteros silently cursing. The 3-wood carried into thick rough, but he then produced what Ballesteros and Jacklin described as the best shot they had ever seen under fire. Torrance delicately flighted a sand iron downwind over a bunker and managed to put it three feet from the hole. The single putt dropped, North could not match it and things were all square.

'On the 18th tee, adrenaline pumping, Torrance belted out "the best drive I've ever hit", then watched in delight as the shattered North skied his drive into the water. "I knew then I had won," said Torrance. "I am not afraid to admit I cried all the way down that final hole. What a feeling!"

'After missing for his five, North stood disconsolately as Torrance, inevitably, rolled in a magnificent 15-footer to win the Ryder Cup in style.'

The next day the *Record* devoted a full page to a feature by John Fairgrieve: 'Should big boys cry?' He concluded that Sam had nothing to be ashamed of – he was in good company. 'Last week at Jock Stein's funeral, some of the hardest men in football couldn't hide their tears and, in the end, didn't bother to try.'

Colin Montgomerie, Europe's biggest money-earner in 1993, has been Scotland's other standard-bearer in professional golf in the 1990s, with a talent capable of capturing one of the majors even though his temperament is sometimes in doubt.

He came agonisingly close to winning the US Open title in 1994 at Oakmont. No Briton has won the American title since Tony Jacklin in 1970. Montgomerie forced his way into a three-way play off with South African Ernie Els and America's Lauren Roberts. But in the 18 holes shoot-out the

man from Troon could only finish third, and Els went on to win at the second extra hole.

In the post-war years it was the combination of John Panton and Eric Brown who carried the flag. Panton, honorary professional at the R & A, was winner of the Scottish Professional Championship eight times. He was the pro at Glenbervie for 38 years, and he played in three Ryder Cups and 12 World Cups. But the peak of his playing career was in 1967, when he beat the famous American, Slammin' Sam Snead, 3 and 2 in the final of the World Senior Championship. Cyril Horne reported from Wallasey on the 50-year-old Scot's triumph against the 55-year-old Snead:

'Panton has rarely ever played with more skill or assurance. He shot 69 in the forenoon round, compared with Snead's 73, and was three up. Then in the afternoon, as the course ran even faster, he continued to control his shots superbly, and was four under 4s for the 15 holes played, just as Snead was. So that for the 34 holes of this highly competitive match, the winner taking £500, the imperturbable Scot was seven under 4s.

'Snead took his defeat with very good grace. Several times he referred to Panton's magnificent putting: "John, I'm sure you're working with radar."'

Eric Brown died in 1986 and in his tribute Alister Nicol wrote, 'A golfing legend died yesterday with Eric Brown. The Brown Bomber was one of the greatest players ever produced by the home of golf, but the game's greatest prize, the Open Championship, eluded him. He twice finished third – at St Andrews in 1957 and then at Royal Lytham the following year, when he needed a four at the last to win but took six, and Aussie Peter Thomson became Open Champion for the fourth time.

Eric's proudest boast was that in four successive Ryder Cup appearances made from 1953 to 1959, he was unbeaten in singles. When his Ryder Cup playing career ended he was appointed skipper in 1969 – the dramatic drawn match at Royal Birkdale – and again at St Louis in 1971.

Significantly, Brown said after the '57 event at the home of golf, 'A home Scot will never win the Open in Scotland. There is far too much pressure from the crowd.' Even if the crowd would love a Scot to win there is ample consolation – the Open is now one of the world's greatest sporting events –

Opposite: Colin Montgomery ponders the way ahead.

and Scotland has staged some of its epic clashes. Ben Hogan had a triumphant year in 1953 winning the Masters, the US Open and the British Open at Carnoustie.

The man who put the glamour back into the tournament was undoubtedly Arnold Palmer, beaten by one shot when Australian Ken Nagle won the centenary Open at St Andrews. The American won the next two Opens and in 1962 'Arnie's army' cheered him to victory at Troon, when he finished an amazing six shots ahead of second-placed Nagle.

The first Open I covered was Tony Lema's 1964 win at St Andrews, and we all shared the champagne he sent to the press tent. That's style! For many of us, however, there was no finer Open than the first ever staged at Turnberry, the 1977 head-to-head between Tom Watson and Jack Nicklaus. Alister Nicol wrote:

'An era ended at sunbaked Turnberry on Saturday when Jack Nicklaus failed yet again to win a British Open Championship. It was the sixth time this mighty Golden Bear had finished in second place to add to his two victories. He summed it all up after losing to fellow American Tom Watson by just one stroke: "I gave it my best out there today, but I'm tired of giving this championship my best shots and finding they are not good enough." That was as near a concession as anyone is likely to get from 37-year-old Nicklaus that he knows the young brigade are poised to break down his 15 years of dominating world golf.

'Watson, with two magnificent final rounds of 65, proved for the second time this season that while he regards Nicklaus as the world's greatest and has tremendous respect for him, he is not in awe of the Golden Bear. The 27-year-old held off a late surge by Nicklaus to win the US Masters and, over the closing 36 holes of the greatest Open ever seen, refused to be intimidated.

'Time after time Nicklaus had Watson reeling. But time and again the super-confident psychology student steeled his nerves. In the end it was the once infallible Nicklaus who cracked. He missed a five-foot birdie putt on the 17th to let Watson go in front for the first time – after 71 holes of superb golf. He did rally enough to make a birdie at the 18th – but by that time Watson was sitting only two feet away from the hole and his second Open title in three years.

'I'm not daring to suggest that big Jack is over the hill, but one thing is certain – a new breed of fearless, brash Americans led by the superb Watson is ready to take over.'

Nicklaus wasn't over the hill. He won the following year's Open in a play-off against the unlucky Doug Sanders at St Andrews.

Professional golf now takes up most of the massive space given to the sport, but it was different in the 1930s, when amateur golf also drew huge crowds. Here is Hector Thomson, on Page One in June 1936, as he is carried shoulder-high by the members of Williamwood, Glasgow, after he had won the British Amateur Championship at St Andrews. 'Allwill' was the pen-name of the *Record*'s golf writer of the time, Willie Allison, who had a uniquely individual style.

'Crack! A moment's pause, then – another crack! In the hushed atmosphere when even the birds in the heavens seemed silenced, twenty thousand eyes followed the flight of the two white pellets which flew from the tee towards the last green of the hallowed links of St Andrews. The sound of club striking ball reverberated over that stretch of green.'

He then went on to describe 22-year-old Thomson's second shot which gave him victory against the 21-year-old Australian, Jim Ferrier.

'As the ball was struck, our necks were suddenly jerked towards the emerald green of the putting surface. In a beautiful rainbow-like arch the ball careered. It landed safely in the harbour, and stopped six inches from "port". There was a gasp of astonishment. Then a wild cheer of acclamation. A dream shot, which will be talked about when we are all greybeards, and the other highlights of this memorable championship are dimmed in our memories.

'The young Scot gained the crown by two holes for the first time since J.L.C. Jenkins, as a home Scot, triumphed in 1914. It was almost like the last chapter of a fiction thriller. Never has the coveted British title been won in such dramatic fashion and never by such a glorious effort.'

Thomson and his friend Jack McLean were the big names of Scottish amateur golf in the 1930s. But in the women's game,

Jessie Anderson, later Mrs Valentine, was just as famous. 'Wee Jessie', daughter of a Perth golf professional, had helped halve the 1936 Curtis Cup against America at Gleneagles when she holed a putt on the 18th green to win her tie.

A year later, aged 22, she won the first of three British amateur titles, and Allwill acclaimed her 1937 victory:

'Hats off to Miss Jessie Anderson, Britain's new golfing queen. A great champion, a great golfer and as fine a little lady as has ever gone seeking golfing glory against the most powerful women players in the world. A crowd of over two thousand paid homage to her yesterday when, in the final of the British Women's Championship at Turnberry, she emphatically mastered Miss Doris Park, the Scottish champion, by 6 and 4.'

Dunlop advertised their famous '65' golf ball on the same page at 2s (10p) each!

Mrs Helen Holm from Troon also won twice in the pre-war period, and in the 1960s smiling Belle Robertson, from the golfing outpost of Dunaverty in Kintyre, went on to win top honours in Britain, including the Amateur title in 1981, and captain Curtis Cup sides.

There was a 21-year-gap between Hector Thomson's win of 1936 and the next Scotsman to take the British Amateur title. The *Record* reported in June 1957:

'Scotland's smallest golf club went wild with excitement yesterday. Almost every member, and hundreds more, turned up at Dullatur clubhouse to welcome home Reid Jack, the new British Amateur Champion.

'And what a reception they gave him as he walked into the clubhouse, proudly holding the British Amateur Championship trophy. The miners, farmers and businessmen who play with Jack every other week crowded round to thump him on the back. The huge silver trophy was filled with whisky, and filled again. And when the new champion told them, "I will be proud to go representing Dullatur," their cheers nearly lifted the roof.'

Reid Jack beat American serviceman Harold Ridgley 2 and 1 in the final at Formby, Lancs. The wait was even longer for the next Scot to lift the trophy. It wasn't until 1992 that 18-year-old teenager Stephen Dundas won the title, the first time in 35 years it had been won by a Scot. The paper said:

'The gangling 6ft 3in Glaswegian wrote his name into the

history books when he scored a magnificent 7 and 6 triumph over Welshman Bradley Dredge in a sun-drenched final at Carnoustie. Afterwards Dundas declared: "Augusta here I come!", for as Amateur champion, he receives invitations for both the US Masters and the US Open.

'The teenager, who had once been a target for Celtic, came from the Haggs Castle Club in Glasgow. He had studied at a college in Texas, and although he had not won a trophy in three years he said: 'This is not a bad way to end my drought. That was as good as I could play under pressure. I have not surprised myself, but I am certainly relieved.''

Stirling University student Gordon Sherry came so close in 1994, losing 2 and 1 to Englishman Lee James in the final at Nairn. Sherry, a 20-year-old 6ft 8in giant weighing 17 stone, promised Alister Nicol: 'I know I'm not nearly good enough yet, but there's a lot to come from me in the future.'

Ronnie Shade never won the British title. But he certainly dominated Scottish amateur golf for a spell, with five straight wins between 1963 and 1967. R.D.B.M. Shade – the initials stood for 'right down the bloody middle', rivals were known to remark – had such a stranglehold that the paper even devoted a page after what turned out to be his last victory on whether his monopoly was in the best interests of amateur golf.

That was after he had beaten Alan Murphy by 5 and 4 in the 36-hole final at Carnoustie in 1967. Cyril Horne said: 'Having won the championship five times and established a record that may never be equalled, Shade is entitled to think that there is no reason why he should not make the number of successes six, seven or even eight times in a row.'

He in fact failed to add to his trophy tally, but he occupies a place in Scotland's golf hall of fame besides so many illustrious names. Humble hackers like myself can only regard their achievements with awe.

Auld Enemies

Scotland v. England at Wembley

It was born in 1924 and it died in 1988, but no fixture had a greater impact on Scotland's football fans this century than the bi-annual clash with England at Wembley. Victory or defeat there was felt much more keenly than at Hampden Park. As soon as one match was over, the weekly savings in pubs, clubs and workplaces began for the next visit to England two years away. The Wembley weekend became a ritual that was enshrined on the nation's football calendar.

For the real fan it didn't matter how you got to Wembley, or even if you had a ticket. All that counted was being there, as my former colleague, Jack Adams, found out on one trip south in the 1970s. He got talking to one fan in the buffet car of the night train south to Euston. The supporter, in full tartan regalia, brought out a wad of notes to buy a drink and then informed Jack he would be getting off at Carlisle. When asked why he wasn't going any further, the fan replied, 'I never pay the fare. It's a matter of family honour. None of us have ever bought a ticket to get to Wembley. They'll find out at Carlisle I haven't paid, so I'll just get off and get the next train.'

And, sure enough, two days later in the crowd at Wembley the same fan hailed Jack, another trip south completed!

The origins of games between Scotland and England, the

It's the era of the Wembley Wizards. This team, in 1929, defeated Wales 4–2 at Ibrox. Back row (left to right): Jackson (Huddersfield), Muirhead (Rangers), Harkness (Queen's Park), King (Queen's Park), McPhail (Rangers). Front row: Blair (Clyde), Gallacher (Newcastle Utd), McMullan (Man City), Dunn (Everton), Morton (Rangers), Gray (Rangers).

world's oldest football international, go back to 1872 and a 0–0 draw at Hamilton Crescent in Glasgow.

The venue for the fixture changed frequently, and it wasn't until 1906 that in Scotland it found a permanent home at Hampden Park, and settled there until the end of the line in 1989. But in England it took 20 more years before the Football Association settled on Wembley Stadium as the home of the game against Scotland. The first match was played there in 1924, but even the fixture two years later between the near neighbours and deadly rivals went ahead at Old Trafford.

However, on a wet Saturday in March 1928 a soccer legend was born: Scotland's mighty midgets, dubbed 'The Wembley Wizards', grew into football immortals by sweeping to a 5–1 victory against the might of England. As with so many of our international successes, the Scots had been written off before the game. The *Record* reported the view of SFA president Robert Campbell before the game: 'I am very confident of victory and I don't agree with the opinion expressed in some quarters that our side is deficient in power.'

But the paper's writer 'Waverley' (John Dunlop was the first to use the pen-name), could not completely disguise his fears, although a stiff dose of patriotism made sure he didn't actually say England would win:

'Today Scotland's chosen sons will go down fighting at Wembley, or come back with honour. Look at the chosen side through the most patriotic of glasses you can get hold of, and you will, if you are a discerning Scot, admit that the odds are against us.'

He touched on the fears that the Scottish forwards were too wee: 'Let us hope that our Lilliputian forward quintette – four of them stand about five-and-a-half feet – will find a hole in the Saxon armour.' He was obviously sitting on a very large fence as he wrote hopefully:

'Haven't Scots teams, which seemed to have less chance of winning than this one, gone down to England and triumphed. Remember 1922, remember Birmingham. Surely Scotland never was represented by a more abused side and of course the players chafed under the severe criticism.

'Captain Jamie Blair assured us when he joined the party: "We have a good side. Those of you who want a flutter on the quiet can make a bit of money, they are offering 2 to 1. We can beat them." History records how this discredited side won that afternoon on Villa Park. They went into the fray with abandon, and scored the only goal of the match.'

I don't think the SFA would take as kindly to the current skipper of the Scottish team offering the same advice to his men to put a bet on themselves.

Among the 80,000 spectators at Wembley in 1928 were ten of the players who had taken part in the 1900 international at Celtic Park and marked the start of the new century with a 4–1 win. It was called the Rosebery international. The Scotland team wore the primrose and pink racing colours of Lord Rosebery, the Honorary President of the SFA, whose horse, Lada, had won the Derby the year before. The *Record* of 9 April 1900, reported, in the style of the time:

'At the close of play Lord Rosebery entered the dressing-rooms in the pavilion and was introduced to the players. He heartily congratulated the Scotchmen on their score and to the Englishmen he did not forget to extend sympathy. All the players were proud of having had the honour of a personal interview with his Lordship.'

That team were known as 'The Old Invincibles', and just to show it's not only football but the meaning of the English language that's changed, it was said they had 'A gay dinner. Each member of the party looked hale and hearty. Under the splendid leadership of Mr R.S. McColl they are in for a grand weekend in the Metropolis.' No doubt it was made even better by the result and the performance of the team made up of

Harkness (Queen's Park), Nelson (Cardiff), Law (Chelsea), Gibson (Aston Villa), Bradshaw (Bury), McMullan (Manchester City), Jackson (Huddersfield), Dunn (Hibs), Gallacher (Newcastle), James (Preston), Morton (Rangers).

By Monday the result made sure there was no doubt about the performance. 'SCOTS WHA HAE ON SODDEN WEMBLEY', said the paper in its largest type, a full half-inch high. Waverley's doubts were swept away. 'Ower a' oor ills victorious,' he happily burbled. But he did have the grace to admit: 'I need hardly tell you I did not look for a Scottish success, and, if the truth were told, very, very few people did.'

However, Waverley had not been well enough to travel to Wembley. His colleague, 'Quarrybrae', filed the main match report, and the customers were given it in dollops, four columns of closely-packed type. Winger Alex Jackson, with Scotland's first international hat-trick since R.S. McColl's in 1900, took the main spotlight and Alex James scored the other two. Yet it might have gone against Scotland in the fatal first minute:

'Nelson made his only slip, an unavoidable stumble on the greasy ground, and Smith strode clean through with the ball under perfect control. It seemed that Scotland were destined to be faced right away with a deficit. Great was the joy, therefore, when Smith's shot, fired from 10 yards' range, rebounded into play from the far upright.'

But in a few puffs of the cigarettes most of the spectators smoked it all changed when Jackson scored the first goal then James the second just before half-time. Then came that superb second half hailed as an exhibition by the Scots as perfect as football will ever be.

'Their power and virility were amazing and the Saxons were lashed and licked into a perturbed state by the warmth of the Caledonian attacks. They were lucky not to have twice five goals registered against them.

'From first to last James was the mainspring of the forward line. No other outside-forward was so effective as Jackson. Morton's centring was beautifully judged and it made three of the goals possible.

'Dunn contrived to keep Jackson on the move. Gallacher was full of courage and the magnificent play of the line was in no small measure due to his expert distribution. The defence put up by Bradshaw, Nelson, Law

and Harkness was stonewall. I have never seen such stylish wing half-back play than Gibson and McMullan.

'Happy are the thousands who made the journey south to view the greatest of all matches. It was wonderful football, and I didn't welcome the final whistle.'

It's not been too often, especially in recent seasons, that many of Quarrybrae's successors in press-boxes round the world could produce such purple prose about Scotland's international side.

The Wembley cult was established. Not even three straight defeats in the years between 1930 and 1934 could change that. There was better fortune in 1936, when 19-year-old Hearts inside-forward Tommy Walker scored from a penalty, even though the ball blew off the spot three times in nerve-shredding succession.

By 1938 the bi-annual trip to Wembley had spread itself not only across the sports pages but onto Page One of the paper as well. The issue of Saturday, 9 April 1938, led with an

Queen's Park captain Bob Gillespie, the last amateur to play for Scotland's full international team, leads out his squad for the 1933 international against England. Called in only three days before the game, he was made skipper, and Scotland won 2–1.

Meet the players: King George VI is introduced to Malcolm MacDonald by skipper Matt Busby at a 1944 wartime international at Wembley.

exclusive hand-written message from Scotland captain George Brown to *Record* readers, helped no doubt by the fact he was a cousin of the Editor, Clem Livingstone. It was reported that a hundred special trains had left Scotland carrying 50,000 fans to London for the Wembley encounter. At Glasgow Central Station there was a vivid description of the departing fans:

'There were tartan glengarries, tammies and scarves, tartan rosettes and ribbons, tartan dolls and tartan umbrellas and even one or two tartan kilts.

'Wildly tartaned excursionists, each with his brown paper parcel of provisions in bottles, chanted inarticulate war-cries, spectators bellowed encouragement as trains steamed out and there were, of course, the slightly alcoholised gentlemen who insisted on singing "The Wells of Wearie" and "Loch Lomond".

'Many of them had been saving up for this for months. They were going to get full value out of it, and they started getting that value as early as possible.'

Two fans even interrupted their bus journey to Wembley at Gretna and shortly before midnight were married over the anvil. The driver of the bus and a female passenger were the witnesses. The groom, Mr John Mathie from Greenock, said: 'When we started out we had no intention of getting married, but when we came to Gretna we made up our minds on the spur of the moment.'

It's not recorded if they made the game, to see Tommy Walker score the goal that proved to be the winner in a 1–0 victory. But Bill Shankly, the man who was later to be manager of Liverpool, growled: 'If we had got a second goal in the first half we would have got a barrowload in the second half.'

It's always tempting to look back at teams packed with great names in the history of the game and put on rose-coloured spectacles. Surely an international with such stars as Bill Shankly, George Brown and Tommy Walker in Scotland's line-up, and Eddie Hapgood, Stan Cullis, Stanley Matthews and Cliff Bastin in England's team must have produced a fabulous encounter. But Waverley (by this time the acerbic W.G. Gallagher), did not agree: 'It was a deserved victory, but it was not a game to be labelled international standard.'

The paper also reported that the SFA were unhappy about the ticket distribution for the game, but secretary George Graham said: 'Two years from now the holding capacity of Wembley will be greater and the number of tickets allowed to Scotland will be correspondingly bigger.'

But ominously, even with so much sports coverage, there was an item dealing with Prime Minister Neville Chamberlain talking in a speech in Birmingham about the threat of war. And two years on, there was no Wembley in 1940; the world had a more bloody conflict to concern itself with by then – the first months of the Second World War.

The first Wembley clash after the War was a 1–1 draw in 1947, but it was the 1949 international which took its place in football's Hall of Fame. This was the era of newsprint restrictions, with the day's events squeezed into tiny 10-page papers. The *Record*, rather primly, listed the Scottish team with their full names: James Cowan (Morton), George Young (Rangers), Sam Cox (Rangers), Robert Evans (Celtic), William Woodburn (Rangers), George Aitken (East Fife), William Waddell (Rangers), James Mason (Third Lanark), William Houliston (Queen of the South), William Steel (Derby County), Laurence Reilly (Hibs).

They were up against an English team packed with top names such as Billy Wright, Stanley Matthews, Stan Mortensen, Jackie Milburn and Tom Finney.

The Wembley Wizards were invoked with a message in

It's 1941 and Britain is at war. But unofficial internationals are still held, and Prime Minister Winston Churchill meets Jimmy Caskie at Wembley.

the paper reminding readers: 'The odds in 1928 at Wembley were almost the same as they are today. Scotland was given little chance by the bookmakers – but they forgot about the odds.' The invading Scots army was up to the size of pre-war crowds and this time the paper reckoned 'At least 4,000 Glasgow hopefuls made the 16-hour dreary trip by bus.'

It was nearly 1928 all over again, as Scotland swept to a 3–1 victory and the next day an incredible crowd of 10,000 fans stormed Glasgow's Central Station to greet the returning team. The *Record* said:

'As, 85 minutes late, the *Royal Scot* rounded the bend into Platform 11, a Hampden roar shattered the silence of expectancy. Goalkeeper Cowan was the hero of the hour and from those 10,000 throats rose the chant "We want Cowan, we want Cowan!"'

Waverley summed it up:

'In the good old days we used to "name" our internationals with England. We had Bobby Walker's game, Andy Wilson's game, Hughie Gallacher's game, and so on down the years until 1938 when, by reason of a magnificent match-winning goal, we called in Tommy Walker for the christening ceremony. But then we came to a sudden stop.

'Since then our teams have been of such a mediocre calibre there hasn't been much competition among the players for the honour – until Saturday. And I reckon that in future years, when the thrilling victory is recalled, the game will be spoken of as a personal triumph for Jimmy Cowan, the keeper who was very nearly not chosen.'

It was indeed Jimmy Cowan's Wembley. In the finest 90 minutes of his career he produced a series of spectacular saves to foil England. Jimmy Mason put Scotland ahead in the first half, followed by second-half scores from Billy Steel and Lawrie Reilly.

'Our third goal was a picture effort. Waddell got away on his own and 20 yards out he cut in. If ever a ball was placed on a man's head it was Waddell's cross to Reilly and the Hibernian dealt with it in masterly fashion.'

Bob Ferrier, whose first visit to Wembley it was, reported that at the end of the game the Scots fans swept on to the pitch.

'No barriers built could restrain them. They were over the dog track, over the speedway track, over the touchline and over, in a flood, the Scottish team.

'And for goalkeeper Cowan something special. They bore him shoulder-high from the arena and if that young man ever again has such a supreme moment of sporting ecstasy in his life, I cannot imagine it.'

The royal guests of honour were Princess Elizabeth and the Duke of Edinburgh. When the Princess, now the Queen, was asked who she was supporting, *Record* readers were told she answered, 'Scotland, certainly.' The Duke said, 'England,' with a smile. But at half-time, with Scotland leading by Jimmy Mason's goal, the Duke had changed his mind. 'I think I am supporting Scotland now,' he said.

Scotland did well in 1951 with another win, and a late goal from Lawrie Reilly – 'Last-minute Reilly' – gave them a draw in 1953. But there was the first of a series of Wembley disasters in 1955, when England won 7–2. Mercifully, a newspaper strike at the time robbed readers of the cruel details of the match. Scotland right-half Tommy Docherty recalled: 'It was the greatest goal I ever scored, and it was greeted in deadly silence. We were 7–1 down when I scored with a free-kick. But we were so far behind it made no difference.'

Docherty was speaking in the *Record* of 15 April 1961, the day when an even greater disaster struck Scotland. The nation reeled in collective humiliation from a score-line that read England 9, Scotland 3. Waverley had gloomily ended his preview with the words: 'I think we'll be doing very well indeed if our fellows go back to their dressing-room without suffering defeat.' However, skipper Eric Caldow had been upbeat. 'We'll all be in the dumps at anything less than a clean-cut victory.'

The paper also reported the threat of Italian clubs snapping up top players from Scotland and England. Jimmy Greaves of Chelsea was going to Milan and Denis Law of Manchester City and Hibs' Joe Baker were also likely to move to Italy.

But that story was swept away by the Wembley result in which a Scotland side, strong enough on paper, had been put through the shredder. The team was Haffey (Celtic), Shearer (Rangers), Caldow (Rangers), Mackay (Spurs), McNeill (Celtic), McCann (Motherwell), McLeod (Hibs), Law (Manchester City), St John (Motherwell), Quinn (Motherwell), Wilson (Rangers).

George Young leads out the Scotland team, on a trip to nowhere. They lost 1–0 to England and failed to clinch the British title. The SFA said they would only enter the 1950 World Cup if the Scots were home international champions.

217

A bare-foot lap of honour, having beaten England at Hampden, 1962.

Thumbs up from a Scotland fan to Davy Wilson, Willie Henderson and John White after Scotland's 1963 Wembley win over England.

The preview had said of Celtic keeper Frank Haffey: 'He has only to give us a sample of his best club type of game to justify to the full his inclusion.' But Haffey was only one of many flops in the side. No wonder he eventually emigrated to Australia. And Waverley's wrath was directed at the seven selectors who, in those days, picked the team and then handed it over to manager Ian McColl: 'I say that Scottish football was disgraced, and the chief responsibility for the blushes of over 30,000 Scots must lie squarely on the shoulders of the selectors.'

But two years later the irrepressible Scots were on the Wembley trail again, and full of hope. This was the first England-Scotland match I saw, so it remains my favourite Wembley memory.

It was a reshaped Wembley stadium, with a splendid new press-box which sadly is no longer in use for journalists. And from our roof-high eyrie we saw one of the dramatic matches in the history of these clashes. The day before the game Rangers left-half Jim Baxter had told *Record* reporter Jim Rodger: 'If I don't play well here I'll quit the game. What perfect conditions for a footballer.'

They certainly were, for Scotland suffered the loss of captain Eric Caldow with a broken leg after only five minutes.

No subs in those days, so his Ibrox team-mate Davy Wilson went to full-back. And Scotland, with two goals by Jim Baxter, romped to a 2–1 victory.

That set up an even greater victory at Wembley four years later, when the Scots dumped the 1966 World Cup winners for the first time since they had been crowned champions. By this time the *Record*'s main sportswriter was the ebullient Hugh Taylor, who brought a much-needed modern touch. Before the match he warned:

'England are, must be, a better-balanced more composed and more seasoned team than Scotland. But we have Law and Baxter. They are, I declare, our main hopes. But they'll have to leave their temperaments at home. They want to lick England, really lick them. For these dashing adventurers are loyal Scots and proud – also sad that England and not their own country are World Champions.'

Still, even Taylor, always the optimist, thought it wise to add a final caution: 'If we lose it certainly won't be for lack of fighting spirit or courage.'

But by Monday it was yet another Wembley when all the pre-match fears seemed ultra cautious as Taylor hailed Scotland's win in his own inimitable style. The Scots had powered to a wonderful 3–2 win, with goals from Denis Law, Bobby Lennox and Jim McCalliog. And Taylor, always happier when hailing victories, surpassed himself:

'Scotland were magnificent arrogant masters of Wembley, contemptuously humiliating the once-proud World Champions. I am only sorry now that the 3–2 score wasn't what it should have been – 6–2.

'Scotland revealed style that will go a long way in helping us win the World Cup in 1970, and we must praise manager Bobby Brown for that.'

Alas, that was one prediction we are still waiting to be fulfilled. It didn't happen in 1970, or any other year. Team boss Bobby Brown lost his job and Hugh Taylor departed for the great press-box in the sky, leaving a vast empty void here on earth where the man's style, both in his writing and his life, are still greatly missed. But that day in 1967 was one of the golden afternoons of Scottish football, as Taylor summed up:

'Perhaps it isn't football, never mind cricket old boy, to tease and torment opponents like this. But I loved it. I

Joy at Hampden: John White gives Jim Baxter a piggy-back lap of honour after the 1964 1–0 win over England.

219

Close shave for England, as Jimmy Johnstone fires in a shot in the 1970 Hampden clash, with Alan Ball (left) and Emlyn Hughes watching.

Bobby Lennox strikes a superb goal despite the efforts of Bobby Moore.

Wembley at 4.50 on 15 April 1967. Scotland have just beat World Champions England 3–2, and the Scots fans celebrate with an invasion of the pitch.

The moment that rocked Wembley: police wrestle with a Scots fan who threw a punch at England's Alan Ball (third from left), 1973.

Trouble flares. Scottish and English fans clash in a Hampden brawl.

Spot the ball: Dave Watson of England and Scotland striker Joe Jordan battle it out.

England's Kenny Sansom competes with Gordon Strachan for the ball, 1980.

loved every moment of it. And even in the press-box, that haven of neutrality, there were cackles of Highland delight as a tartan dream of glory came true.'

And, with 1967, an age of innocence at Wembley passed. An age when the game, and the footballers who played in it, made the headlines. As I've shown, the fans who made the pilgrimage were vital parts of the Wembley weekend. But by 1977 it had all turned rather nasty. Scotland won 2–1 and it sparked off a crowd invasion. The cross-bars and goalposts were smashed, the turf ripped up for souvenirs. Typically, Alex Cameron pulled no punches on the Monday after the game:

'The shame is that rampaging fans also did damage which cannot ever be repaired. We should be talking today only about the superb way Ally MacLeod has introduced himself to international football. The fans are the reason we have other things to talk about. They should be abjectly sorry for their smear on a very fine team performance.'

The solutions came thick and fast. They tried mid-week matches in an attempt to cut down on crowd trouble, and two consecutive games at Hampden. And then 1988 brought down the final curtain at Wembley for the game against Scotland. Few folk now remember the score, a 1–0 win for England from a Peter Beardsley goal. The headline on a blunt Page One message from the *Record* was: 'FORGET IT'. And the paper added, 'Wembley isn't worth all this.' It reported how a 19-year-old fan from Bishopbriggs, Glasgow, had had his face ripped open with a Stanley knife and how a 25-year-old London policewoman lost two front teeth and suffered a suspected broken nose. A Scot was accused of attacking her. It also spotlighted how battle-scarred Scots fans endured a night of terror at the hands of Nazi English soccer thugs.

There was one more match against England the following year at Hampden, and after more crowd trouble it really was the end of the line. It was the only sensible decision. The fixture had to be stopped as public order considerations overrode football.

Yet the marvellous memories of the great Wembleys can never be forgotten. Sometimes I can close my eyes and see again one of those wonderful tartan-tammied fans, perhaps ever so slightly the worse for wear, hear his chorus of 'Wembelee, Wembelee!' and recall when we really did have games to celebrate.

Next page: Is this one worth more than the World Cup? Joe Jordan and Tom Forsyth hold aloft the Home International Championship in 1978, watched by Colin Jackson, and front Derek Johnstone and Danny McGrain.